The Last Things We Talk About

Your Guide to End of Life Transitions

Elizabeth Boatwright,
DMin, BCC-PCHAC, CFP

Bull Publishing Company
Boulder, Colorado

Bull Publishing Company

P.O. Box 1377

Boulder, CO USA 80306

www.bullpub.com

Library of Congress Cataloging-in-Publication Data

Names: Boatwright, Elizabeth, author.

Title: The last things we talk about : your guide to end of life transitions / Elizabeth Boatwright, DMin, BCC-PCHAC, CFP.

Description: Boulder, CO : Bull Publishing Company, [2021] | Includes bibliographical references and index. | Summary: "Whether we like it or not, we all die. People avoid talking about death because it is too mysterious, too dark, and occasionally, as in the case of an accidental or other sudden death, too unpredictable. Because we do not discuss death and dying in our current culture, people are left to wrestle with large questions about death. This book is a place to start thinking about, and preparing for, this inevitable event. The primary goal of *The Last Things We Talk About* is to help readers affirm, celebrate, and remember the people and experiences they cherish in this life. It encourages them to seriously consider their death and take planning one step at a time, according to their schedule, and as energy permits. Elizabeth Boatwright, DMin, BCC-PCHAC, CFP is a Relief Chaplain in Oncology Outpatient Palliative Care Medicine at Stanford Health Care. She has over 25 years in ministry experience serving diverse cultures along with extensive work in the arts and financial planning"--Provided by publisher.

Identifiers: LCCN 2020048001 (print) | LCCN 2020048002 (ebook) | ISBN 9781945188350 (paperback) | ISBN 9781945188367 (ebook)

Subjects: LCSH: Death. | Death--Planning.

Classification: LCC HQ1073 .B63 2021 (print) | LCC HQ1073 (ebook) | DDC 306.9--dc23

LC record available at https://lccn.loc.gov/2020048001

LC ebook record available at https://lccn.loc.gov/2020048002

Printed in the U.S.A.

26 25 24 23 22 21   10 9 8 7 6 5 4 3 2 1

Interior design and production by Dovetail Publishing Services

Cover design and production by Shannon Bodie, Bookwise Design *to Frank*

Guide to Key Pages

If you or someone you love has recently received a serious/terminal diagnosis, turn to pages 7, 10, 12, 59

If you need to facilitate conversations about end-of-life matters with loved ones, turn to pages 20, 23, 26

If you want to identify meaning and purpose in your life and learn how to tell your story, turn to pages 9, 12, 50

If you need more information on the health care system and continuum of care, turn to page 31

If you are looking for housing alternatives that accommodate aging populations, turn to pages 29, 33

If you are downsizing/moving or helping a loved one move or pack up a home, turn to page 45

If a friend, family member, or loved has received a serious/terminal diagnosis and you want to know how best to support them, turn to pages 121, 131

If you are planning a funeral/memorial for yourself or someone else, turn to page 157

If you are looking for digital, virtual, or ecological options relating to end-of-life issues and burial plans, turn to pages 97–101

If you need to learn more about body disposition options, turn to pages 80, 95, 142, 152

If you need to get your end-of-life financial/legal paperwork in order, turn to pages 75, 88

If you have been asked to be a health care proxy, turn to page 75–76

If you have been asked to be a personal representative and would like a checklist, turn to page 148

If you want to learn more about end-of-life practices in other cultures, turn to pages 221–234

If you are losing, or have lost a loved one, and are working though the mourning process, turn to pages 170–174

If you have medical bills and you need help understanding them, turn to pages 71, 73

Contents

Acknowledgments

As this book has been over 15 years in the making there are countless people to acknowledge:

To my amazing family: husband, Frank; sons, Stephen and Floyd, and their families; my sisters and brother, Sally, Suzanne, and Dave, and their families. You are, along with Christ, the rock I stand on. Without your prayers and support, this book would still be in a box waiting for someone to say yes.

To the original team of the class "The Last Things We Talk About" at Lake Grove Presbyterian Church, Pastor Bob Sanders, Ron Bailey, JD, and Frank Boatwright, LCSW, who laid the groundwork for the book.

To the more than 800 participants at Lake Grove Presbyterian Church in Lake Oswego, Oregon, and First Presbyterian Church of Sunnyvale in Sunnyvale, California, who helped to critique and shape the class over the past 15 years.

To friend Patty Moorhead who developed the manual inventory "Final Wishes" to augment the work in the classes.

To Rev. Dr. Dan Chun, my mentor, and his spouse, Pam Chun, founders of Hawaiian Island Ministries and leaders at First Presbyterian Church in Honolulu, Hawaii.

To those consultants and readers who assisted in review and accuracy: Rev. Petra VanderWater, The Venerable Zhiyun Cai, Mahesh Bhavana, Bill Futornick, Chaplain Taqwa

Surapati, and Fr. Randy Valenton, Peter Johnson and Dr. Christine Keeling.

To department chair Lori Klein and the chaplains in Spiritual Care and the social workers, doctors, AP nurses, administrators, counselors, and technicians in Palliative Care at Stanford Health Care for their continuing compassion and trailblazing work in caring for the seriously ill inpatients and outpatients we all love.

To those who did say yes: author Dr. Kate Lorig, the catalyst who introduced me to Jim Bull; editors Erin Mulligan and Julianna Scott Fein; and the staff at Bull Publishing. Thank you. The adventure is just beginning.

Introduction

Whether we like it or not, we all die.

Some of our bodies are placed in the ground with a solemn ceremony, some cremated into ashes with a short eulogy followed by a wake or a good party. Still others may be transformed into an ice cube for eternity (or until a cure is found). In our modern Western world, we have found every conceivable way of not talking about death because it is too mysterious, too dark, and, on occasion, as in the case of an accident or a sudden death, too surprising and unpredictable. Talking in general about anything serious may be on the decline, as many of us have become devoted exclusively to social networking at the expense of face-to-face conversations. And with the continual decline in church, mosque, and temple attendance, more and more people are left to wrestle with questions about death without any knowledge of the traditions of our ancestors or any idea where to start.

So we brood over our approaching demise, assuming we have no power over the time, place, or way we will meet our end. Some of us pay for every conceivable potion and lotion to retain our youthful glow or figure, only to discover that under our youthful guise, our internal workings and health are in decline and we are out of balance. We ponder the countless movies and novels on the mysteries of death. We may puzzle over the romantic Western inclinations of the nineteenth century to die by suicide or the burial traditions of various indigenous cultures.

But we often still can't find what we are looking for. And, especially as the millions of baby boomers approach their retirement years, the following become all too common questions: How do we do this thing called death? How do I put "my house in order"? What's next after a loved one dies?

This book is for people who are looking for answers to these questions. It is for people who may be near the end of their lives, as well as the people who are surrounding these people and who love and support them. As our parents die in our arms or in hospital rooms, as a pandemic swirls around us globally and threatens our livelihood and futures, we are fearful. For those of us who are perched on the upper tier of adulthood, the reality of death is staring us in the face. There is an urgency to prepare our blueprint for leaving this land called life and to forge our path into our own legacy.

I would like to help you answer these questions for yourself. I have been counseling and guiding people through this landscape for over 35 years. Along the way, I've been fortunate to navigate many different professions, and each of them has helped me learn about people and how we live and die. I taught disadvantaged children in an age of bussing and unrest. I managed unruly tenors and diva sopranos at the San Francisco Opera. I survived market crashes and turbulent buyouts of investment firms as a certified financial planner. I pastored a congregation of 1500 and presided over more than 30 memorials a year. My time as a pastor included unforgettable moments, such as the time I almost fell into a grave on an icy morning, an instance where I nearly tripped over and upset a poorly placed jar of ashes in a church, and the day I managed to escape unscathed from a food fight prompted by an angry family's inability to agree on how to handle mama's service.

I've also buried both my parents and a sister-in-law. My current role as a palliative care and hospice specialist at Stanford University Hospital focuses on offering intimate bedside service with a culturally sensitive presence, prayer, and purpose. What you have in your hands is the summation of all those experiences. I have written this book to serve as a manual of how to manage life in a time of diminishing returns and emotional upheaval.

I've divided this book into seven chapters that are best read in order. Chapter 1, "Exploring and Expressing Meaning and Purpose," is a journey of self-discovery. I wrote this material to help you to identify what is important to you and to articulate what gives your life meaning and purpose. It also aims to assist in identifying the people who make up the concentric circles of support in your life. Chapter 2, "Making Wishes Known to Loved Ones," is about communication with family and all the people you love. I want to help you figure out what you want to convey to them about your wishes, transitions, support, and the legacy you wish to leave. Chapter 3, "Talking about Health and Illness," covers medical conditions and the continuum of care. And very importantly, it introduces two key documents: a durable power of attorney for health care and an advanced directive. In the discussion in chapter 3, we walk through what you need to have in place in terms of these permanent health-related documents and how to get your health affairs organized. Chapter 4, "Putting Your House in Order," further discusses decisions you need to make and additional documents you will want to gather and distribute to loved ones. It also gives advice on how to locate the professionals who can assist you as you put together the needed inventories for financial, legal, and practical matters.

The last three chapters of the book will be especially important for those who have lost a loved one or are in the process of losing a dear one. It is for the survivors who are picking up the pieces of their lives. Chapter 5, "Saying Goodbye and the Dying Process," explores the rituals and celebrations of the end of life. Chapter 6, "Figuring Out What Happens Next," outlines the practicalities that need to be taken care of after someone dies. Finally, chapter 7, "Piecing Things Back Together after Death: Conversations around Grief and Loss," centers on the emotions surrounding death and how survivors can cope.

My job is to be your guide. I am sort of a death docent. I will lead you through the maze of questions that death engenders and resources to help you to answer these questions. I will also encourage you to relax and take things one bite at a time, on your schedule and as your energy permits.

When we have finished our journey together, it is my hope that you will have drafted an archive of important documents, a guide that your family will be able to use to follow your wishes when you die, or that you will have discovered some positive ways to help you care for an aging or ill family member. Either way, my primary goal is to help you affirm, celebrate, and remember those whom we cherish in this life. I look forward to walking alongside you.

1

Exploring and Expressing Meaning and Purpose

We begin to find and become ourselves when we notice how we are already found, already truly, entirely, wildly, messily, marvelously, who we were born to be.

—Anne Lamott

For you created my inmost being; you knit me together in my mother's womb. I praise you because I am fearfully and wonderfully made; your works are wonderful, I know that full well. My frame was not hidden from you when I was made in the secret place, when I was woven together in the depths of the earth.

—Psalm 139: 13–15

*The friend who can be silent with us in a moment of despair
or confusion, who can stay with us in an hour of grief and
bereavement, who can tolerate not knowing . . . not healing,
not curing . . . that is a friend who cares.*

—Henri J. M. Nouwen

Sam

Sam sat dumbfounded in the clinic office. His oncologist
had just told him that his inoperable cancer had
metastasized (spread) to his kidneys and liver. His cancer
was now in stage IV. He had a limited chance of survival.
He was facing weeks of chemotherapy and radiation. And
if chemotherapy and radiation could shrink the tumor, he
still faced the possibility of surgery and weeks of recovery.
He would need to determine how to financially afford the
appointments, medications, specialists, hospital stays, and
his visiting family's hotel bills. Sam wondered, would they
wait for him at work? At 44, he was too young; his family
would never accept this. His mind was exploding. He
needed time to think before he could make any decisions.
He began to weep into his partner's shoulder.

Alice

Alice, the 82-year-old survivor of a recent fall, lie in the
hospital. She'd broken her hip and her legs were weak.
Tubes had taken over her body—one for elimination,
another that pumped medication directly to her heart,
and one more for nutrition and hydration. Alice's face
was pale and her heart was not functioning well. Nurses
came in every 15 minutes to check on her, and she was
feeling overwhelmed. Finally, the doctor and her team
entered the room and delivered the bad news: Alice had

suffered a major stroke and there was little hope for a full recovery. She was facing an immediate intervention with a rehabilitation stay of at least six weeks. After that, she would need at-home care and a move might be necessary, as her house was not suitable for living alone post-stroke. Would her daughter take her in? Did she have the finances to manage an expensive alternative arrangement? She had no idea. Her independent life as she knew it was over and she couldn't even remember how it happened.

Your Chapter 1 Checklist:

1. Answer the "What Matters Most to Me?" list of questions.

2. Learn how to recognize potential limits to your energy and to work within those limits to prioritize the people and things that are important to you.

3. Determine who matters most to you and your role in their lives.

4. Identify the concentric circles of support in your life.

As these stories show, a life-altering medical diagnosis is like falling off a dangerous cliff without a safety net. If you are at the receiving end of this kind of news, you are in free fall, and unsure how deep or sharp or devastating the canyon is below. And at the end of the fall, you have to find your way out through an uncharted path to the reality of a new normal. In these stories, both Sam's and Alice's lives are forever changed and their priorities, expectations, and dreams will need to be realigned as well.

So where do you start the journey to living your life in the wake of hearing a frightening diagnosis? What are the things that matter most? What do you count on to bolster you up when you feel the earth has opened a trap door beneath you? What can you do when you hear a diagnosis, or hopefully even before you hear one, to be as ready as possible for what comes next?

You Are Here

As with any journey, you must start where you are. I work in a hospital where there are literally hundreds of signs. There are signs at elevators and at corners. There are signs in long hallways that feature red arrows pointing to the Emergency Department. Other hallways have signs in diverse colors pointing out the way to various departments. But the one sign that absolutely grounds me is the little star on the elevator sign that is labeled, "You are here." If you are lost, or unsure of where you are, you begin to find your way by finding that star. The star begins the journey. You can look at the star, realize where you are, then find your destination and decide how you will get there. Similarly, you need to find the star when you receive devastating or life-altering news. You start at the point of departure and decide where you are headed and the direction you want to take.

But before you begin to plan your route, you need to breathe. If you have just had some bad news about your health, get a handle on your emotional temperature and take some time, maybe a few days or more, to absorb the news before you begin to plan. Talk to a trusted friend or spouse, a confidant who knows you and has your back. Take a walk or a hike. Touch the earth and experience it with all the senses you have. And for a moment simply "be" without any agenda. Pray and meditate. Allow the ideas, the deep sorrows, the hurt, the regret, the insane feelings, and the tears just spill out. When you hear difficult information, you need this. Not only for your sanity but because these moments are catalysts for greater thoughts and plans. You may want to write down what you are feeling or hearing from your inner spirit.

Like Sam, you may have been hit with hard news about your own health. Your life is playing out like a scene from a bad movie and no one is directing. You can't comprehend that just a few days ago you were planning a trip to a favorite vacation spot. Now you stand to lose your job, your livelihood, any discretionary income, and your relationship with your family as you know it. This reversal of fortune is too much for quick comprehension. This is all the more reason for you to take a break and get some perspective. Decide what matters to you and set priorities on how you will move forward.

Or maybe you relate to Alice or to Alice's family. Not only is a loved one ill and devastated, but you are facing the possibility of altering your life to be a primary caregiver for a person who may not want your help. Maybe it is a parent who has always been fiercely independent and only this year gave up driving. Your mother or father or a grandparent has been living a predictable and ordered life, and neither you nor they can imagine how this new paradigm of surgeries, rehabilitation, and doctor visits is going to work.

Whether you are facing a diagnosis, supporting someone else who is, or are just ready to think about the future, if you are reading this book, it is time for you to focus on what matters. The information in this chapter will help you do just that. Let's take a walk together and discover who you are.

What Matters to You: Identifying Meaning and Purpose in Your Life

As a chaplain who specializes in palliative care and hospice, I see countless patients who are making their way through their lives and managing their affairs as if on autopilot. Their jobs are reasonably stable, their family is managing well, they have a few supportive people around them, and there's enough money in the bank to get through every month. Everything seems okay until a life-threatening diagnosis. Then life hits the breaks. Now priorities, meaning, and purpose are overheating their personal engines, and they are in uncharted territory without a map. I have written this book in an attempt to help you avoid being one of those folks. It's time to chart an alternative route.

My suggestion is that you begin this journey deciding what matters most. I'm hoping you took that walk in the woods or by the seashore and had some time to just be. Now it is time to focus on what matters. You need to figure out what gives your life meaning and purpose. To help you do that, ask yourself the questions in the "What Matters Most to Me?" questionnaire below. You can find a blank copy of this questionnaire in worksheet form in the appendix on page 204 as well.

▬▬ Questionnaire: What Matters Most to Me? ▬▬

1. What matters most to me? (*What comes to mind first when I read this question? For example, is it my spouse or partner, family such as my children and grandchildren, my faith, my profession, my friends, a cause? When I read this list, which response resonates most for me?*)

2. What brings me joy? (*What wakes me up in the morning? What inspires me to keep going each day? What are the tasks, programs, activities I love? What restores me? What brings me hope?*)

3. What do I hate/I avoid?

4. What has helped me in the past to get through difficult times? (*What are my best coping mechanisms? Is it sleep/rest, avoidance, prayer, checking in with family, asking loved ones for help, calling a friend, trying something new such as a new hobby or skill, exercising, cooking, walking, or what?*)

5. Are there upcoming milestones (*anniversaries, birthdays, graduations, vacations, births, celebrations*) or dates that are important for me to be present for or important events I want to attend?

6. Who depends on me? What kind of things do I provide for those people? Are there other people who can take on these responsibilities if I am no longer here?

7. What scares me right now? (*What keeps me up at night?*)

8. What are the things I want people to know about me? (*Or in the words of Anne Lamott, what makes me "truly, entirely, wildly, messily, marvelously" who I was "born to be"?*)

9. What am I on Earth? What is my purpose?

10. If I get through this time, what would I like to change about me, my life, my community, my world?

Answering these questions truthfully and completely may take a while, but it's worth the time. As you respond to the questions, you are defining who you are, your hopes, goals, gifts, fears, and joys. As you fill in the worksheet, the things that matter most come into focus. Once you have these questions answered and you have identified what gives your life meaning and purpose, you can pause, breathe, and appreciate how you are fearfully and wonderfully made and begin to map out your next steps.

Where Did Your Energy Go?

If you are facing a disturbing diagnosis, all the mental processing and goal setting you are doing may leave you feeling depleted or exhausted. Some people describe a serious health diagnosis as like a kick in the gut. It can be physically debilitating, emotionally draining, and mentally challenging. Trying to get your head around the diagnosis, prognosis, treatments, stress of appointments and support groups, medications, finances, inactivity, and lack of sleep or nutrition creates mental and physical exhaustion. Add to that the needs of your family, the worry and uncertainty, the stress of dealing with insurance and other financial concerns and there simply isn't enough of you to go around. Give yourself lots of permission to say "no." The self-care of rest and non-scheduled time is a gift.

To figure out where you should and should not spend your energy, take charge with a large black marker and a calendar. What part of your daily regimen needs to be rearranged or abandoned based on your treatment schedule? Do you really have to go to every sports and theater event or can you take a pass? And who are the folks eager to help?

This can be a very good time to determine who matters in your life, identifying your concentric circles of support, and assigning your understudies. Figuring out what matters and who matters and delegating tasks to support people are important first steps to take after a diagnosis.

Who Matters to You and What Is Your Role in Their Lives?

Here's a tough question: Who would miss you or your support when you are no longer alive? You would probably start with your spouse or partner, then your children and grandchildren, and then round out the list with your parents or siblings. For many people, next are close friends. Then there might be close business associates and those you supervise at work. All of these people matter.

The next question is: What role do you play in each of their lives? Are you the sole breadwinner in your home, a caregiver, parent, supervisor, boss, mentor, or special friend and counselor? And if you are no longer around, what tasks would still need to be addressed? If you are a parent with children still living at home, it might be providing an income stream for your childrens' expenses, advising and nurturing their growth and development, and facilitating decision making and special activities. You may also care for a child with special needs. Who will handle their Individual Education Plan (IEP) if you are absent? Do you have someone who could be appointed an advocate if there are other legal or medical matters to address? If you are a child of older parents, you may need to find an alternative to your caregiving and visits. Who will do this for your parent(s) if you cannot? If you have business responsibilities, you may consider a business continuation plan that assigns tasks and creates job descriptions.

Worrying about these people who matter might keep you up at night. Think about who matters and what they need from you. Make plans to address those needs in your absence now while you have the energy. Hopefully, you won't have to put the plans into action.

Identifying Your Concentric Circles of Support

I often think of people and the folks in their lives in terms of concentric circles. The first circle centers on the primary person, you—all your warts and moles, spiritual core, eccentricities and faults, giftedness, joy, and achievements that are both tangible and intangible.

The second circle contains those trusted family and friends who are the "2:00 a.m people." They are the ones who understand all the components of who you are. Even at 2:00 a.m. in the morning, you can call on these people when you are in crisis, have a need, or want to share unspeakable triumphs or sorrows. They are the people whom you trust with your secret concerns, your BHAGs (Big Hairy Audacious Goals), and your most intimate confessions. Not surprisingly, there are often some people in this circle that are not family members.

When the crisis hits, the members of this second circle will be able to take the news about your diagnosis and sit with you and work it through. They can offer wisdom without lecturing or judgment and remain silent until you are done explaining the state of your heart and soul. They take the time to walk in your shoes, show empathy and compassion, even in the most complex of situations. This team is the "be" crew; the non-anxious folks who don't have an agenda. They are the people who are content to just be with you and do not feel compelled to rush to fix a situation or do something. They are the people who walk beside you.

The third circle is made up of trusted people and advisors and other family members. This can include spiritual advisors, good friends, counselors, clergy, and medical professionals who understand and care about your situation. Although not as connected to you as those in the second circle, they are people who understand you personally and professionally. They have a good idea of what is best for you because they've taken the time to know you. This group is the "do" team. They are doers because they are generally goal- and task-oriented. With little direction, they can help you formulate and get through a to-do list. These are the people who will set up goals for your recovery and healing, organize a team for delivered meals, run errands, make sure you make time for physical exercise, assist in securing mental and emotional wellness resources, and offer prayers and spiritual comfort.

The fourth circle is made up of more geographically distant relatives, your acquaintances, and the professional practitioners in specialty areas who are paid by the hour or program. The fourth circle also includes neighbors, fellow parents you know from your kids' sports teams or school activities, as well as folks whom you engage with by permission or appointment, such as lawyers.

The fifth circle includes pretty much everyone else except those you do not trust. It is sometimes necessary to identify those you do not trust, because with documents such as an advance directive for health care you have an opportunity to declare those you do not want to grant permission to make health decisions for you. For some, that might be a former spouse, a shady relative (you know, the less-than-honest or even criminally minded relative), or a relative who simply has never gotten to know you. When you are in a crisis, the medical team at a hospital tries to reach the people you have designated on your advance directive. If you have not completed an advance directive, then they will look for next of kin. If you have a parent, child, or close relative listed anywhere in your personal database, they will attempt to contact them first.

It is good to have an inventory of support people. As you construct your inventory, you can decide which groups and which individuals need to be included in certain decisions and which do not. You may even want to assign specific tasks to people as you think of them. As noted earlier, figuring out the things and people that matter and identifying support people is an important step to take after a diagnosis. You are a unique and wondrous being. Take care of you. Then take the time to talk to your loved ones.

2

Making Wishes Known to Loved Ones

Your story is what you have, what you will always have. It is something to own.

—Michelle Obama

You are going to feel like hell if you never write the stuff that is tugging on the sleeves in your heart—your stories, vision, memories, songs: your truth, your version of things, in your voice. That is really all you have to offer us, and it's why you were born.

—Anne Lamott

Who lives, who dies, who tells your story?

—Lin Manuel Miranda

Frederico

Frederico's family was determined to be his team. Taking time off work and finding child care with relatives and friends, twenty of them crowded into his already modest hospital room to hear what the doctors had to say. Working through a translator, the doctors presented the difficult news. Frederico's kidneys and liver were shutting down and the possibilities of recovery were slim. Frederico was the sole provider for his spouse and five children. Relatives were already making plans to care for his three sons and two daughters for the duration of his stay so his wife, Blanca, could stay bedside. Family members stayed in touch and regularly called relatives to come and visit the hospital. Some stayed the night in the atrium with blankets provided by the staff, while others kept vigil in the waiting room with snacks and TV.

Each evening, they held a family meeting/potluck dinner at Frederico and Bianca's house to catch up on the news and pray for a miracle. When the end was near, they remembered his requests. They called the priest for reconciliation and anointing, and the family gathered around Frederico's bed. This gave him a chance to tell each of them, one by one, how he felt, and what they meant to him in his life. He wanted to tell his story. Then they prayed the Rosary, the Our Father, and the Gloria Patri. This was what he had wanted and planned for—family and friends, blessings, prayers, and a chance to say the things that mattered. Frederico's family was open, willing, and available to carry out his final wishes.

Billi

As wonderful as Frederico's story is, things don't always work out that well. There are some families and cultures that are less open or even completely closed to talking about medical issues or health challenges. Maybe you are in a family that believes just talking about the illness creates a self-fulfilling prophecy. Perhaps you and your family members prefer to remain stoic and silent in the face of death. Or you may have relatives that believe avoidance will make it less emotionally painful. Some families also feel that discussing things like this outside of the immediate family is taboo, and that discussing these topics openly is akin to disloyalty or dishonor.

Perhaps one of the best examples of this family dynamic is in the 2019 movie *The Farewell*. The Conversation Project® (a public engagement initiative with a goal to have every person's wishes for end-of-life care expressed and respected) describes the film this way: "In the movie, we're introduced to Billi—a young Chinese American woman who is conflicted when her family refuses to tell her terminally ill grandmother, Nai Nai, that she is dying of lung cancer. This fascinating movie enlightens viewers as it reminds us that how we deal, discuss, and engage with death/dying is deeply influenced by our culture. We are called by this movie to consider how one's culture greatly informs the way they approach issues of end-of-life care."[1]

In the film, Billi can't understand why her family won't tell Nai Nai what is going on. It frustrates her that she has to go along with the ruse of inventing a fake wedding to get everyone together one last time to see her grandmother.

Old stories and resentments surface, family secrets are revealed, and everyone tries to cope the best way they can without revealing the real reason they flew into Hong Kong.

Your Chapter 2 Checklist:

1. Plan and have a conversation with loved ones about key decisions relating to health and aging.

2. Look into extended care living options and research their costs. Discuss and decide on best options with your family.

3. Make an inventory of items to give to loved ones and make plans to dispose of the rest.

4. Figure out how you want how to tell your story and collect what you need to share your history and legacy.

This chapter is about family and communication, how a family can talk and work together to sort out housing, care, and wishes for the end of life with cultural sensitivity. It covers ways to tell your story and focuses on letting family know who you are and what you want. The common thread in both Frederico's and Billi's stories is that every family has its own communication style and rules. Talking about sickness and mortality can be tough, embarrassing, or even improper in some circles. So how do you get everyone to the table to have the discussion we all need to have?

Getting Everyone to the Table and Having Productive Conversations

I have been in conference rooms with a family similar to Frederico's and watched 20 to 25 family members negotiating with a doctor about their loved one's care. I've witnessed other discussions where family members adamantly assert that they expect a miracle. Some family members cannot conceive of a negative outcome. Sadly, the people or families that stand to lose the most in terms of health care are those that try to deny the truth, not willing to stray from their cultural or religious sensitivities and family "rules."

Doctors and medical professionals will do everything medically possible to save the patient or cure the illness unless they are mandated to do differently by you or your family. So you need to have conversations with your loved ones to agree on what you, the patient, and your family want to have happen. If your family does not want you, the patient, to know what is happening, you may have to appoint an advocate who acts as a spokesperson for you as the patient and a mediator for the medical staff. If this is what needs to happen, there are many tools and programs to assist you that you can find in the appendix at the end of the book. Some good options are introduced in this chapter.

The Conversation Project and the Stanford Letter Project

The Conversation Project is a national program designed to ensure that end-of-life care wishes are expressed and respected. Most families, if asked, would love to have a conversation about end-of-life concerns but don't know how to begin. The Conversation Project wants to make it easier. The project encourages you to answer a simple set of questions and discuss these questions with the relevant parties over coffee, dinner, or at some other appointed time. The questions cover end-of-life issues such as how and where a person wants to be treated, the kind of medical procedures they agree to, as well as general questions about wishes and hopes. Families may feel skittish or unwilling to discuss these topics. The intent of this Conversation Project meeting is to allow participants to talk about hard questions without feeling inhibited. It also allows the patient a chance to engage in two-way conversations.

For example, family members who are part of the Greatest Generation, born before the end of World War II, may refuse to have the conversation. It may not be a topic their family of origin addressed in their formative years during the Great Depression. They may believe they are giving up their independence by sharing and delegating end-of-life concerns and are loathe to depend on someone else. In that case, they need to be gently guided and encouraged to tell their truth and discuss what matters to them. The Conversation Project's inventory of questions simply gets people to the table.

The Conversation Project also offers a wealth of additional resources: bibliographies, card games, podcasts, information on financial and other professional services organizations, and health care resources. Starter kits are available to download and print for free at https://theconversationproject.org/starter-kits/.

The Stanford Letter Project is another innovative program. Developed by Dr. VJ Periyakoil, it encourages individuals to write a "What Matters Most" letter (in any of eight languages) to their physicians stating their personal preferences about end-of-life topics. Topics include: what matters most to me at the end of my life, my important future life milestones, how we prefer to handle bad news in my family, how we make medical decisions in our family, who I want making medical decisions for me when I am not able to make my own decisions, what I do not want at the end of my life, what I do want at the end of my life, what I want if my pain and distress are difficult, and what to do when my family wants you to do something different than what I want for myself.[2] Recently, a Life Review

Letter was added for friends and family that covers seven tasks: acknowledging people in your life, remembering key moments, forgiving others, asking for forgiveness, saying thank you, saying I love you, and saying goodbye. Visit their website for more details at https://med.stanford.edu/letter.html.

Conversation Stimulus Activities and Games

There is no one-size-fits-all approach to making wishes known to loved ones. Activities such as card games can also stimulate conversations. According to their website, the Funeral and Memorial Information Council (FAMIC) created Have the Talk of a Lifetime to help families have important conversations about the things that matter most to them and how a person's life story can be remembered and honored in a meaningful way. Beyond the many downloadable activities they offer, they have conversations cards for purchase. In the deck of cards, not all the questions are centered on the end of life, but they ask some probing questions such as, "If you could choose your last words, what would they be?" or "How do you want to be remembered?" and "What words of wisdom would you pass on to your childhood self?" The conversations that these cards inspire are often about wishes and hopes. You can learn more about their activities at talkofalifetime.org.

The Coda Alliance is a community-based, not-for-profit organization with a similar purpose, helping individuals and their families plan and prepare for the concluding passages of life. At their site, you can purchase or play for free online the card game Go Wish. The game has a deck of 36 cards, and it addresses 35 common wishes such as "to be free from anxiety," "to take care of unfinished business with family and friends," and "to maintain my dignity." This game can be played alone or with two or more people. The solitaire game asks the player to sort the cards into three piles: (1) important to me, (2) somewhat important to me, and (3) not important to me. Once the cards are divided, the player sorts through the "important to me" cards and picks a top 10. If there are not 10 in the "important to me pile," the player adds some from the "somewhat important" pile. With that top 10 pile, the player has the means to begin an engaging conversation with family on what matters.

Go Wish is helpful for those who are non-verbal or struggling with communication due to medical procedures. If you want to play in groups, the second (and third person) might be health care agents. Each member puts the cards in the same three categories and compares their picks. You can learn more at gowish.org.

These sorts of activities and games help to express and share perceptions and expectations. Are these perfect solutions? No. But they are simple tools to jump-start conversation among family and patients who struggle to explain and discuss how they really feel. All of these exercises can help prepare family for the inevitable changes and transitions ahead.

Transitioning: Considering and Making Changes

Once a person starts to struggle with activities of daily living (ADLs), such as dressing, bathing, and toileting (see also section "Activities of Daily Living" on page 29), in their home, they and their families may need to find in-home care or face difficult decisions about moving a family member from home to another facility.

For many elders or seriously ill patients, moving to a care facility is distressing and could even be thought of as the equivalent of receiving a death sentence. Some people may fiercely oppose medical advice and family wishes and fight for their independence. They may make family feel as though they have been rejected altogether.

If a patient and a family have discussed needs in advance, there is greater chance that everyone involved can see the merits of supervision over uncertainty and possible accidental death. If these tough topics are addressed early and mutually, difficult living situation transitions are likely to go more smoothly.

It is difficult to have conversations about changing living arrangements immediately after someone has lost their loved one or spouse. The trauma of losing a partner, parent, or child is difficult enough. Instead of leading with moving, it is best to begin with conversations regarding how a person will manage alone and the things family and friends are willing and able to help with (and not help with). This conversation is valuable for all parties. If it is decided that moving into a facility is the best plan, keep in mind that a new community of people in a facility may assist or exacerbate the loss. Before making any moves, visit any potential facility. Go to lunch, sit with the residents, and get a feel for the facility. Then have another talk.

Aging in Place

If you are an independent thinker who insists on remaining in their home, you need to have a conversation with your family and ask them what they will do and not do to assist you. Then make sure to have an emergency plan in place: a first alert button to call five emergency numbers, a completed Physician Orders for Life Sustaining Treatment (POLST) form for the refrigerator, an advance directive for health care completed for the medical team that agents will carry out, and phone numbers for home help. Less abled folks staying at home will also need a list of agencies for grocery delivery and Lyft or Uber accounts or access to special transportation groups who specialize in errands and medical visits (some phone companies have set up services to call the drivers for them). Include in this inventory a list of friends who will come in the case of an emergency.

Some families, mine included, put together a monthly schedule with one person per day checking in on our elder relative to handle appointments and trips. This disperses the responsibility and keeps the family talking as a group about special needs or concerns. Everyone assigned to the calendar needs an emergency sheet of doctors, clinics, family phone numbers, and help agencies. At some point, a family member may wish to create a joint checking account to make sure that finances are stable, bills are paid, and there are no abuses or fraud concerns.

If you or your loved one ages and stays at home, it's likely there will be a need to hire outside assistance at least a few hours a day or overnight if an elderly or disabled person lives alone and there is no one else in the home. This is a form of mental insurance for the family to make sure the loved one is okay.

This home care (cleaning, cooking, errands, general maintenance, and medication management) is billed hourly and is not paid for by Medicare, and it's likely any agency you find to provide care will ask you to commit to a minimum number of hours per day. Before beginning the search for care, decide exactly what hours of the day would suffice, what services are needed, and what resources are available to pay for the help. Take the time to read every part of any contract you sign and ask lots of questions.

You need to be wise regarding whom you hire. Although the majority of the agencies are bonded and licensed, it's tempting to hire someone privately for less. Do not forget there are strict laws governing labor, insurance, taxation, and liability issues. Get references, talk to others who have used the agency, and compare notes.

If a senior's income qualifies for local In Home Support Services, the county of residence may either train and hire a relative (who is probably already working in this capacity) to be an in-home caregiver or offer to hire a person from an agency. There is tremendous stress involved in hiring the right helper, but it's worth all the effort if you find the right person to care for your loved one.

The Multi-Generational Home

In former decades, certain members of the family, generally female, did not work outside the home. Instead, they remained in the family homestead to care for multiple generations. On one level of the home was the growing family of children and on another level, the parents who moved to the home in their later years. The expectation was that the elders would be cared for, as they cared for their children in an earlier generation. Everyone ate together, grandma and grandpa might watch the children when the parents went out and countless celebrations took place under one roof. And when grandma and grandpa got sick, mom stayed home and cared for them or took them to the doctor. There was never a question about who had the responsibility for them in their later years.

In the twenty-first century, in many homes both spouses work to provide income, and the multi-generational house is no longer the norm. The multi-generational home is a paradigm that many of our elders long for, but it is no longer likely they will attain it. Still, some families make it work. If the younger generation has a bedroom with a separate entrance and the amenities of a small kitchen and bath attached to their home or a cottage in the back, living together might be a possibility. It provides autonomy with some supervision. This plan works best if both sides set some parameters or rules and give themselves time off from "togetherness." Boundaries are important for both parties but independence with benefits can work.

One of the toughest realities we currently face in this country is the risk of putting loved ones in a nursing home or similar facility. As of June 29, 2020, 42% or over 59,000 of all US deaths in the coronavirus/COVID-19 pandemic were linked to nursing homes due to a confined environment and workers moving from room to room.[3] Many families have opted to bring their loved ones home to prevent risking their health in congregate care. But elders who have no family nearby have little choice but to wait out the possible consequences. As a result of these new realities, living in the home of a relative or close friend who will maintain a safe, healthy environment is emerging as a preferred and even permanent choice. Some loved ones will require additional in-home support, but the proximity of having that person in close range makes sense for many families in the face of the health risks of group care.

Currently there is a growing industry in accessory dwelling units (ADUs) or units built onto or adjacent to one's present home. Although the up-front costs are more than most budgets can afford, the long-range planning makes sense. If a family is paying $7,000–$10,000 per month to care for a loved one in a facility (depending on where they live), two years of those payments could possibly cover the cost of building this dwelling.[4]

Whatever plans seems to work, there is usually a time when moving out of one's own home or the family home for reasons of supervision, socialization (or mental health), is necessary. In the following sections, I discuss possible options for families in this situation.

When More Care Is Needed

We all fear serious life-changing news about our health. You may be facing a terminal illness that comes with diminishing physical and cognitive ability. Or you may be pondering the news that your life expectancy might be extended if you are willing to go through some clinical trials or experimental procedures. Will there be American Disabilities Act (ADA) equipped facilities available? What kind of after-care will a surgery require? Will your spouse/partner/family be burdened? What's the cost of having in-home support and what kind will I need? Given all the questions you might be facing, it's good to equip yourself with facts about your future care challenges and how to avoid being taken by those who prey on the vulnerable.

If given a choice, most of us would prefer to remain in our homes and receive care from a loved one until we die.[5] But this may be unrealistic. Either your cognitive or physical abilities might prohibit us from an independent life or there may be a lack of family or support to grant us this independence. So what determines if we need to make a transition to more care and how do we go about getting that care?

Activities of Daily Living (ADLs)

If nursing care is required, many health care plans provide for the cost of that care. It is a person's ability to carry out day-to-day activities of daily living (ADLs) that often determine what kind of care is required. Activities of daily living are basic tasks of daily life that able-bodied people carry out without assistance. The ability to perform these tasks helps determine medical status for health coverage and long-term care decisions.

The following is a basic list of ADLs:

- Bathing and cleansing your body and taking care of your personal hygiene (for example, brushing teeth and combing hair)

- Using the toilet independently

- Dressing yourself

- Feeding yourself

- Walking or transferring yourself from a seated position to standing or in and out of a car or wheelchair

To qualify for nursing home care, most facilities require that a person is unable to perform two or more ADLs without assistance. Since nearly half of all us who reach 65 will spend time in a nursing home or require care at home,[6] our ability to carry out ADLs is an important component in qualifying for assisted living. It's highly recommended that families communicate concerns about ADL abilities to one another before disagreement delays the process of getting assistance or threatens the safety of the patient.

But here's the tough news. If you do not qualify for nursing home care through your health care plans, home care is generally paid for out-of-pocket.

In some situations, if a person qualifies for Medicaid assistance, their county of residence can arrange for In-Home Support Services (IHSS) where an aide is placed in the home at no charge for a specific number of hours based on medical needs. IHSS can also pay an hourly wage to a relative to provide the same care. This is often the best solution, as there is often a family member who is already handling this role unpaid.

What are the costs for those who don't qualify for nursing home care through a health care plan or IHSS? Depending on the agency and geographical location, the hourly rate for home care can range from $20–$40 per hour. Multiply that by 8–16 hours a day and you can see why families try to find older retired family members or friends or younger family members without another job to handle the responsibility.

Continuum of Care

Continuum of care describes the delivery of health care over a period of time. For example, in patients with a disease such as cancer, this covers all phases of illness from diagnosis to the end of life. The following discussion describes the stages of continuum of care in the medical world.

Outpatient Care

Outpatient care is typically received outside the hospital setting. Outpatient care includes visits to specialists for assessment and procedures that do not require overnight stays and observation. Outpatient care is a common denominator to most health systems as it helps to cut costs. A more recent add-on to outpatient visits are video "telehealth" sessions and online chats and appointments with medical practitioners, which are now covered by Medicare. These programs allow the patient to remain home without having to ambulate or drive and allow for frequent updates and observations. However, for matters of restricted medicines such as those that involve opiates, an in-person visit is normally required at time of prescription refill.

Inpatient Care

Many inpatients enter the hospital through the emergency department, are under observation for a while, and are then admitted, or they may have a planned surgery and ended up in a patient unit. Either way, an inpatient is assigned to a bed, given a set of specific instructions, and are not allowed to leave unless given permission. In the hospital, visiting hours are limited, a restricted diet (or no food) may be ordered, and a patient may share a room with a complete stranger for a roommate (and all their relatives) for the duration. Medical teams roam the rooms looking for diagnostic clues. An inpatient may need to go in for a series of tests or be readied for an operation or procedure. They are given a period of time to recover before being sent home or on to a rehabilitation center for therapy (neurological, physical, or occupational). A case manager is assigned to patients to inform them of discharge instructions and next steps and what to expect regarding recovery and medications when they return home. Case managers may also educate caregiver(s) on home care and let patients know when to consider returning to the hospital if things are not going well.

Medical Equipment

Hospitals do not provide medical equipment when you check out. Many people assume that their facilities will provide wheelchairs, bathroom chairs/commodes, walkers, and adjustable beds, but that is not the case. You must purchase your own—either new or used. And it can be expensive depending on the model or condition of the equipment you need. Although some doctors can make a case for you to have mandated equipment paid for by insurance, this is rare. Talk to your physical therapist, case manager, or doctor and find out what is required. Prepare to borrow or buy what you need in advance. Check on support groups willing to provide equipment if you can't afford it.

Long-Term Care

Many people's cognitive or physical abilities prohibit them from staying in their own homes and they ultimately need to seek long-term care. If and when that becomes the case, there are a number of options to explore. In the following sections, I discuss some of these options to help family's make decisions about long-term care.

Continuing Care Retirement Communities

At continuing retirement communities (CCRCs) and other so called "graduated step" communities, residents begin with independent living apartments, and then "graduate" to an assisted living wing (or separate building) as their needs change. The final living arrangement is the health care center.

This stepped approach allows residents to age in place without the difficult transitions of moving themselves and their belongings from one facility to another. Many facilities allow residents to pay into an equity system and have a residual investment in the complex and leave a resulting inheritance to heirs. But even in this case, residents pay a month-to-month fee for meals, amenities, and services. Other facilities require that residents make an initial payment to the system without equity and also pay a month-to-month fee.

Facilities offer a host of activities appropriate to age and ability: a regulated amount of nutritious meals served in a common area, graduated supervision of activities of daily living, and a continuing neighborhood of people who share common interests and share transportation and excursions together with those who are no longer driving. A facility like this can often feel like a city unto itself. And with the pride of ownership for those who have invested in the property, there's a shared need to maintain and upgrade the properties with resident councils and boards.

If it fits into a family budget, a CCRC often provides a consistent, stable, and agreeable home for years. Be aware, however, that many of these facilities require that a person have long-term care insurance. For people of advanced age, this can be very expensive. Request a full ledger of costs and fees before signing any contracts. The upside of these facilities is that the sick or rehabilitating do not have to leave campus. Residents are in familiar surroundings near friends and staff who know them and can admit patients to the hospital as merited.

Assisted Living Facilities

Assisted living facilities offer residents their own apartments or rooms and around-the-clock supervision, meals, house-keeping, and laundry, as well as assistance with personal care and medications. Assisted living facilities are a common solution for the person who is no longer able to live alone due to issues with ambulation, driving, and activities of daily living, and who could benefit from supervision and socialization with others. Perhaps the most common candidate for this kind of care is a recently widowed spouse whose partner was a best friend and caregiver and whose children are hundreds of miles away. Or it might be a person whose cognitive and social skills have left them isolated and in need of friends, daily routines, some socialization, and activities. Others may need daily supervision, regular meals focused on dietary needs, and a safe place to live.

Quality runs the gamut. Some assisted living facilities are out of step with the times, but at the same time, other places are updated and well-managed. Check in with friends who have already found a place for themselves or their loved ones, make a map of locations to visit, and always take a standard set of questions to ask when you visit a facility.

Questions to Ask When Choosing an Assisted Living Facility

Questions such as the following may be helpful when touring potential assisted living facilities:

- Who will be checking in with/supervising the resident? How often?

- Who is the supervising agency and where/how can I find out more about their work history?

- Who takes care of a resident who suddenly becomes ill?

- Do you have a physician assigned to this facility?

- Are there registered nurses in the facility?

- What type of care can be provided on site? How is it determined when it is time to be taken to the hospital?

- Are there people available to assist with medications? Is there an extra charge involved for this service?

- Are there provisions in place for residents to move out in the case of a pandemic or health emergency? Will residents be responsible for full payment of fees if they are forced to move out in the wake of such an emergency?

- What is your emergency plan and how are people evacuated?

- Are the rooms cleaned regularly? How often? What are your standards for maintaining a clean environment that prevents the spread of viruses?

- How often to you check the resident's weight and vital signs?

- How often do the residents bathe if assistance is necessary?

- Can you provide a complete list of breakdown of costs?

- How many meals are required/paid for in the plan?

- Do you consult with nutritionists?

- Are there affordable income units in your facility?

- Will residents be given sufficient notice when the rates go up?

- What are the thresholds requiring additional paid care if the person is unable to perform an ADL?

- Do you have skilled nursing facility nearby or included in this facility?

- Do you have a separate memory unit?

- Do you have a physical therapy room, a gym, a movie theatre, a conference room, and a place where my family can have a private meal or meeting?

- Are there beauticians and barber services available to residents?

- Who manages activities and can I see a calendar of sample programs?

- Are "off-campus" excursions and activities included in the fees?

- If they go on outings, does someone from the facility go with them?

- Do you have a list of ombudspersons?

- Do you have rules regarding visitors?

- Are family notified if there is a health outbreak in the facility?

- Are religious services performed on site?

If the person who is planning to live at the facility accompanies family members on a visit to check out an assisted living facility, they will no doubt voice many concerns. Most future residents simply do not want to make the move and will find many reasons to stay in their present home. If your family needs to move a loved one into a facility, do your homework and look for a good opening for the conversation. Speaking with a good friend who has already made the move can be helpful. The times they have expressed loneliness are also important to recall and discuss. Ask about concerns and offer reassurance. Encourage positive aspects such as independence. Work together to figure out ways that they can make time fruitful and pleasant once they are residents of the facility. And most importantly, communicate that ultimately they are in charge of making the decision. Always be firm and kind. Pushing for a decision will only create more resistance.

In a 2020, the annual cost for assisted living ranged from a low of $30,438 in Missouri to a high of $59,400 in New Jersey.[7] An insurance policy that covers long term care or assisted living care may cover the price. However, these types of insurance policies, especially when purchased when the holder is already advanced in years, can prove very expensive. Many people pay assisted living costs with a combination of approaches including paying out of pocket and selling their homes and using the proceeds (minus taxes, capital gains, and expenses for the sale) for living expenses. You may also have the option to tap into Aid and Attendance Pension for veterans. Visit the VestAssist Program website at https://veteranshomecare.com/.

Medicaid can also cover some costs if the facility has specific rooms/beds set aside for Medicaid patrons, but note that Medicaid has both a strict income and asset requirements. Depending on the type of Medicare Advantage program you enroll in, Medicare may also cover some expenses related to long-term care choices. Be aware that Medicare does not pay for the room and board or any non-medical services. Be sure to read the annual official US government handbook, *Medicare and You,* published by the Department of Health and Human Services. You can order it online or make an appointment and receive one at a local social security office. Recently the Department of Health and Human Services added a new online service, *eMedicare,* through their site, Medicare.gov, that provides coverage comparisons, estimated costs for outpatient procedures, and access to your health information.

Rehabilitation Centers/Subacute Centers

It's not unusual for a patient to spend some time in a hospital and then find the next stop is a rehabilitation or subacute center. Hospitals, especially those who are required to follow insurance reimbursements, are encouraged to move people out of the hospital and into a rehabilitation center after a certain period to lower costs and focus on physical and occupational therapy. The belief is that patients will do better after a hospital stay at a rehabilitation or subacute center than they would if unsupervised in their own homes. It also buys some time if you have no one at home who can help and special placement in a supervised facility has been ordered for rehabilitation.

Note that a rehabilitation or subacute center differs from individual skilled nursing. Skilled nursing is a high level of medical care that must be provided by licensed health professionals such as registered nurses and speech and occupational therapists. Examples of this care might include wound care, intravenous (IV) therapy, injections, catheter care, physical therapy and monitoring of vital signs and medical equipment. Skilled nursing care provided in any setting for any duration must be ordered by a doctor to be covered by Medicare, Medi-caid, the Veterans Affairs (VA), or private health insurance. It is possible to receive these services at home, as more seniors choose to age in place, or in assisted living facilities.

These centers vary in quality. One suggestion is to reach out to the hospital case manager as soon as possible and find out where they plan to send you or your loved one and whether or not they have found an available bed for placement. More often than not, you and your family will be given a list of facilities that accepts your insurance plan and a day to choose. If there is time, have someone visit the facilities and interview the management about the schedule of programs and fees. A facility closer to your home or the home of the caregiver is ideal, but recommendations and on-site quality are most important. Seventy percent of adults incorrectly assume that Medicare covers long-term care. In a skilled nursing facility, Medicare covers the first 20 days of each benefit period, a co-insurance amount per day for days 21–100 of each benefit period and all costs for each day after day 100 in a benefit period.[8] Do your homework and know what is covered.

Memory Care

One of the most difficult diagnoses that a family may face is one that involves cognitive impairment and memory loss. A loved one is no longer able to remember simple tasks, daily routines, faces and people, and finds themselves in a "fog" of sorts, trying to find the word, phrase, direction, or thought. It could be that mom or dad's remote memory is in overdrive with endless stories about what they wore to sixth-grade graduation, while their memory for recent information or events is failing or nonexistent.

My dad had both Parkinson's disease and what his doctor believed was a form of Alzheimer's. We were in constant fear of falls, unattended stoves, medicine left in odd places (like the utility room), and a host of other scary events. All our family members took turns helping him, but we were exhausted. This type of care is not a responsibility to take on lightly. Some people, however, find they can manage care at home if they have a caregiver who is strong, able, and possesses infinite patience. In this situation, coupled with some day care programs sponsored by a local senior center or hospital, they might manage. Others find they cannot do the task themselves and begin to look for facilities that handle memory care.

Because the demand for memory care is so high, many assisted living facilities have separate wings that specialize in it. These patients need supervision at a much higher ratio of staff to patients; be sure to check with the administration about how care is managed. Ask specific questions such as: Will one staff member be assigned to three patients or to five? Who is responsible to ensure that the patient eats, toilets, bathes, dresses, and socializes? As you might guess, the cost for memory care facilities is much higher than assisted living due to the increased need for costly patient supervision. Recent estimates for this kind of skilled care facility are between $7,000 and $12,000 per month depending on location and quality.

Palliative Care

There is some confusion about what constitutes palliative care. Let's begin with a definition. To *palliate* means "to ease or relieve." In most cases, what is eased or relieved is pain. Many people associate palliative care with end-of-life care. However, palliative care is essential to anyone with a chronic disease or terminal illness, and many medical professionals believe it should be offered starting at the time of diagnosis. Palliative care is best when it progresses hand in hand with curative care, but because of insurance restrictions and the naïve notion that anyone on palliative care is on a fast track to die, this care is often denied. It might be suggested only when the patient is near death or has no hope for recovery. Some practitioners feel that by recommending palliative care they are "giving up" on the patient and the relegating them only to "comfort measures."

This team of palliative specialists should be thought of as complementary to the primary care team and not a last resort. Palliative care professionals can work alongside the general practitioners or specialists and palliate specific symptoms (like nausea, depression, shortness of breath, or pain). Palliative care also addresses the patient's psychological, social, and spiritual needs so the patient can retain a decent quality of life while they are undergoing chemotherapy, radiation, a pharmaceutical trial, extended illness, or surgical procedures.

The other unique quality of palliative care is that it is comprehensive and interdisciplinary. Typically, a palliative care team is made up of a doctor and/or a nurse practitioner, a social worker, and a chaplain. Each team member is a specialist in their own field, offering physical, emotional, psychological, and spiritual care while working collaboratively with other primary care and specialist doctors to bring about the best possible outcome.

If you or your loved one is receiving palliative care, keep in mind you or your family is still in charge of getting to the clinic or hospital. This may prove a hardship when family members work and there are multiple visits to arrange. You may need to budget for special transportation to get to the facility. Families may also be concerned for the patient's safety in transit and will want an advocate to be with the patient while receiving palliative care. Be sure to discuss the appointment schedule together and keep an updated, shared calendar with loved ones.

Hospice Care

Hospice care is part of the spectrum that includes palliative care but is administered much later in the progression of disease or illness. Traditionally, hospice care is ordered by the physician when the patient's death is likely to occur within six months or sooner. At this point, a patient's condition no longer warrants curative care such as surgeries, emergency room visits, blood transfusions (although there are exceptions to this), or curative treatments such as chemotherapy, radiation, or any other extensive procedures designed to attack or cure the disease. Instead, the emphasis is on comfort, elimination of pain, and emotional stability. Hospice care works with the patient's family and caregivers to communicate about what can be done before death. When receiving hospice care, the patient remains where they are, and the practitioner comes to them and communicates directly with the caregiver.

Medicare covers hospice, so if the patient is over 65 or qualifies under Medicaid standards (normally two years of continual illness and disability and financial hardship), the basic program is free of charge. And what does this include? The hospice team of professionals is similar to the palliative care team. Services may include 24/7 phone visits with an advice nurse, medications, oxygen, a hospital bed and toilet, and regular scheduled visits with a doctor or nurse practitioner. They may also offer home care (such as bathing, dressing, mobility assistance, basic house chores, errands, or companionship) or respite care (giving the caregiver a break from their normal routine) and a social worker to assist with housing and counseling. The chaplain can offer spiritual refreshment and inspiration along with religious rituals as needed. Every hospice service offers a specific menu of options and visitation protocols, so be very specific in your selection and get a full list of what is paid for and what expenses are out-of-pocket.

Comfort Care

Comfort care is the final stage in the spectrum of end-of-life care that includes palliative care and hospice care. It is ordered for a patient in the last days to hours of life. Symptom management is less important than allowing the body to rest and die in peace. Although there are countless options, one option is to decide to find a simple way to keep a patient pain free, dry, and comfortable. This may involve a morphine drip from an IV or liquid drops on the mouth, hydration through sips of water or ice chips, or compresses to the head to ease the heat. Families may opt to ask caregivers to provide a salve for the lips as breathing becomes more labored. There will probably be a catheter for elimination or a simple diaper and chux pad. Hopefully, there will also be music, readings, prayer, and companionship, so the patient will not die alone. There are some wonderful groups like the Threshold Choir that provide music at end of life as well as the nationally recognized organization No One Dies Alone that provides volunteer companions to sit with the patient. Both groups mentioned have chapters throughout North America and local chapters can be found online.

Paying for Long-Term Care

Although many people believe they will not need long term care, current statistics indicate that 70% of those currently turning 65 may need some form of extended care in their lifetime,[9] and Medicaid generally won't cover long-term care until your assets are almost depleted. Costs for medical care, equipment, supervision, and additional fees or coverage can create financial hardship, even to the point of bankruptcy. Most long-term care insurance programs are prohibitive in price except for the few sold through employee plans that may or may not have a continuance clause once you leave the company.

Non-reimbursable home care is $25–$40/hour with some discounts for overnight and weekend stays. An assisted living situation is a minimum of $2500 per month and can cost $5000 per month. Memory care is $7,000–12,000 per month with additional fees for attendants and personal aides. Based on national averages, two years of home care, one year in an assisted living facility, and one year in a nursing facility could cost as much as $191,000.[10] And that's just home costs. There are also the medical procedures to consider. If you are in cancer treatment, the average costs for treatment can run in the $150,000 range.[11] With deductibles, copays, and a good insurance policy, the bill can still be just north of $4,000.[12]

Most financial planners recommend having at least six months of expenses saved in the bank and readily accessible. They also say it is best to have extra saved up if you have a chronic condition that may become a terminal illness at any time. That's the minimum, and it can be a real struggle to achieve. It's never too early to create a savings account for such expenses. If you are still working, set aside an amount each month to create a cushion of support either through a Health Savings Account (HSA) at your workplace or a simple bank account. You may be fortunate enough to receive gifts from family or others to assist. Or, if your partner or spouse has not worked before or is no longer working, they may wish to take some part-time work to defray expenses. If you can afford the help of a financial planner, they may have additional ideas on resources and tax planning to assist you. If you are unable to afford professional consul, the Financial Planning Association (www.financialplanningassociation.org) has no cost or *pro bono* planners available. I discuss more about how to find the right professional in chapter 4, "Putting Your House in Order."

Communicating about Your Possessions: Estate, Online, and Garage Sales

With transition comes adjustments, including deciding what will fit in a new place. At some point, tough decisions about downsizing need to be made. In many people's lives, there comes a time to clean out parts of the past and begin a new chapter of life.

As the third daughter in a family of four children (my brother was the caboose, arriving 13 years after me), I had a lot of "hand me downs" from my two older sisters. I was told that this was twice the blessing and asked who was I to complain? Still I wanted new things, things that were just mine. The used items and somewhat tattered and repaired outfits just didn't cut it for me, especially in my teen years. Yet my closet was full and I could cull the unwanted pieces if I chose. And so it often is with legacy items. Recipients can choose what to keep and what to discard, and this applies not just to physical items such as furniture, clothes, and housewares, but the emotional and psychological things as well.

The definition of the word *legacy* is "something received from an ancestor or predecessor or from the past." In other words, these are the ultimate "hand-me-downs" from our friends and relatives, or what I call "stuff." Yes, some of your things will be handled by the lawyers in probate court or be addressed within a trust. But you can avoid spending money to have other things sorted and inventoried by deciding to take care of "stuff" ahead of time. Spoiler alert: As you have often heard, you cannot take it with you. There are no U-Hauls following the hearse. Eventually everything has to go.

So you might ask, when do I begin this process? My answer is simple. As you are able, begin now. So often an illness depletes you of the energy it takes to handle such a task. Take some time now and create a timeline to begin the project. The traditional ways of culling possessions are estate and garage sales or online markets such as eBay. Whatever you choose, sorting through your possessions will require some focused time. Set aside one or several full weekends or even take some weekdays off from your job to do this work. Sorting through possessions can be emotionally draining. If no one is up to the task, there are many companies that specialize in sorting and managing estate sales. Beware that they will often take 30% or more of the proceeds. If time is limited and finances are not an issue, their services may be something to consider.

First decide on the special things that you want to give to loved ones and then go through everything that is left. Useful categories for sorting include essentials and four tiers of other items. The following list explains further:

- *Essentials.* If the person is still alive and downsizing, what do they need to live? Essentials typically include clothing, medical equipment, bed/bedding/towels, toiletries/medications, kitchen items (silverware, a few plates, a few pots and pans, microwave), window/wall coverings, TV and electronics if they are using them, and financial/office items such as bills and tax and estate records. If the new location is a bare room, you may have to move a few pieces of furniture and decorative items as well. After the essentials are reserved, what's left over is up for sale or donation to family or charity.

- *Tier-One Estate Items.* This category includes china, serving ware, silver or formal dining items, full sets of formal linens, furniture pieces in excellent condition, musical instruments, vases, and original art works that are one-of-a-kind items. If you plan on an estate sale, a family member or selling agent must advertise and get the sale in front of the public. Any extras or leftover items may be put up for sale at the tier-two item garage sale.

- *Tier-Two Garage Sale Items.* This category includes clothes, shoes, coats, hats, hardware, tools, books, CDs, DVDs, kitchen items including dishes, bedding, linens, toys, games, bikes and other exercise or sporting equipment, non-antique/precious furniture, patio and outdoor items, wall hangings and decorations, and plants. In general, think of the lawn and garage as the local discount supermarket. So you don't have to mark everything, apply pricing across categories. Be generous with pricing. Perhaps the proceeds can fund the assisted living arrangement, contribute to the college fund of a grandchild or a special charity, or be kept for the legal costs to settle the estate.

- *Tier-Three Online Sale Items.* This category overlaps a bit with estate sale items and may include one-of-a-kind items, collectibles, special editions of publications or antique toys, etc. Selling online involves taking and uploading photos and shipping. You often have to wait for the sale. Ebay and Nextdoor are two places to start exploring your options.

- *Tier-Four Junk Items.* This category is self-explanatory. It includes items without meaning or value: outdated newspapers and magazines, worn-out clothing (recycle please), items that are dirty and useless, combustibles (take to the proper recycling site for an eco-burial or disposal), and non-reparable things. Junk dealers roam neighborhoods and many cities have once a month special haul outs for these unwanted items. There are even places that accumulate "scrap" items (such as the one in San Francisco called "Scrap") where people can sell and buy cast-offs by the pound.

Purge life of things that are not necessary or meaningful. Think like the popular de-clutter maven, Marie Kondo, who in her now famous book, *The Life-Changing Magic of Tidying Up: The Japanese Art of Decluttering and Organizing*, advises people to hold the item and check in on how they feel. If an item doesn't "spark joy,"[13] move it out. Eliminate clutter. Make room for things that bring purpose and meaning to your life.

The sooner you think about this, the easier the process will likely be. If it is your turn to downsize or you are the one assigned to move Mom or Dad into senior housing or assisted living, what stays and what will you toss?

Santa Claus on Four Wheels: Gogi's Gift Truck

When my grandmother Lucille ("Gogi" to the grandkids) was ready to move into assisted living, she wanted to make sure her family received the items they wanted. With my Aunt Pat's assistance, she made a huge inventory of all her furniture, glass, silverware, and memorabilia. Each of her children and grandchildren were given the list and told to pick their top three items. Once she sorted out the selections, a mover loaded all the items on a big truck and was told to stop at the homes of the children and grand-children. There were to be no arguments. And by the grace of God, there were no duplicates and everyone got the items they wanted plus a few more if the extra items "went" with the requested item. For instance, I longed to have my grandmother's dresser. Lucky for me, her brushes, mirror, buttonhook, powder box, and shoehorn came along with it. Everyone was thrilled that they had a piece of the family homestead in New Rochelle. And my grand-mother was a winner since she didn't have to listen to anyone argue over the prized antiques and possessions. She got rid of her things and died content that she had blessed her children and grandchildren. Yes, there was the cost of the truck, but there were no estate sales or legacy arguments handled by a lawyer. The case was closed and her estate was simplified. Every time I enter my guest room I think of her generosity.

When my last surviving parent died, my siblings and I did the same as Gogi. We drew up an inventory and picked our favorites. There were no arguments, just a wonderful time of memories and laughter. For example, my brother's top pick was a baseball stadium blanket he had shared with dad and a Pinocchio waste basket! Surprises never cease. I'm aware many families may not be blessed with this congeniality. To prevent any arguing among survivors, some people, my husband and I included, make up a list and assign the items. It is such a gift to your family to get ahead of the curve and prevent the fights.

Communicating about
Your Life: Telling Your Story

We've addressed attitudes, choices, and preferences for housing; the costs of care; and sorting out possessions. These are the things a family normally wants and needs to know about when a person is sick or nearing the end of their life. But how do we communicate with others about our story? Part of end-of-life communication for many people involves communicating a personal history and story to loved ones. I love the quote from former First Lady Michelle Obama, which I cite at the beginning of the chapter, but particularly this line: "Your story is something to own." When a family member tells a story, they connect us all to a piece of history.

My Mother's Story

My mom had a fascinating life. She was born in November of 1919. When she was at the tender age of five and a half, her father was shot point blank in Way, Mississippi. His widow, my grandmother, was desperate to find a partner who would care for her and her three young daughters. She married, had a fourth daughter, and subsequently was abandoned by her second husband. For months, my grandmother, whom we called "Big Mama," stayed with relatives and tried to piece together a living on her sixth-grade education. She sold hamburgers on the street and cleaned homes—anything that would put food on the table. But in 1929, at the height of the Depression, times were especially tough and sympathetic relatives were unable to help. Big Mamma finally had to give up her two middle daughters to an orphanage in Natchez and kept the baby with her. The eldest daughter was sent to reform school where she was abused and later married at 14 to escape. My mother was one of the middle daughters.

In contrast to her mother and older sister, Mom thrived. The orphanage found a sponsor for her, she finished high school with honors, and became the pianist for her local church. She took her first train to Houston to attend nursing school and later met my dad (again on a train) during World War II. After raising four successful children and winning countless awards for her music and nursing work, she could look back on her life and say she was a survivor. She wasn't afraid to own her story and proudly declare she'd overcome insurmountable obstacles. When she died, we started a foundation in her "honor" and personally thanked the children's home where she lived as a child.

I am who I am because my grandmother and my mom never gave up. Their story is the beginning of my story and how I have lived my life.

When it is time to tell your story, take the time to record what happened in your life and how it shaped you. It will be both an inspiration and a living gift to the next generation. Here's a few ways to capture the history.

Legacy Box: Consolidation of Memories

One of the more popular ways to consolidate memories is a digital library of photos, films, and memories called a legacy box. Although you might prefer tangible items, boxes of papers and memorabilia are often impossible to sort out or identify once a person dies. My suggestion, as time permits, is for family members to help gather the memories, and sort by year or era with your loved one. That way, if they are able, a loved one can relate stories one-on-one, and family members can record, tag, and digitize memories and memorabilia. Boxes can be transformed into a few DVDs or flash drives. This can also assist the family if someone is assigned to create a slide show at the memorial. Get started on this as soon as you can. While people are still living, this can serve as a way to put some memories together for anniversaries, reunions, milestone events, or a family history.

It's true that a picture tells a thousand words. What a loving gift to sit and hear the back-story of that funny photo with all the relatives lined up on the dock of Lake Winnipesaukee in their '30s era bathing suits, or to get the real scoop on why Aunt Mable married so many times.

Written Memoirs

Another kind of memory building is the written memoir. A memoir may be written down era by era and can be self-published. A sample outline might looks like this: grandparents' and parents' backgrounds, birth, infancy, school years, college, military service, professional life, marriage or adult single life, children, travel, hobbies and avocations, grandchildren, and later years/retirement. It might make sense to include a full chapter on what matters most to you. Was it your faith, philosophy, or vocation that has added meaning to your life?

A memoir like this may offer you and your family member closure and a way to impart the stories that would be lost forever. And as one who has crafted and spoken at hundreds of memorials, I cherish this kind of writing. Your history is a wonderful way to get to know your family. *New York Times* best-selling author Brendon Burchard has a wonderful piece called "Life Interview Guide." It consists of 32 questions that cover the formative years, parents and grandparents, relationships, success and adversity, siblings, parenting, meaning, and purpose.

Verbal Memoirs

StoryCorps is a national program that tapes half-hour sessions about a special time or meaningful events in a subject's life. These tapings occur in libraries, hospitals, museums, cultural centers, schools, or government facilities, and many of the results are then sent to the Library of Congress for archival purposes. If you participate, you receive a taped copy of your recorded memories. If there is no StoryCorps in your area, you can create your own "life scan" of a history. Set up a digital recorder or online voice recorder and use the same outline that is listed in the previous section for written memoirs. To keep it from becoming tedious or tiring, record a series of half-hour tapings. If the subject matter or recorder finds it too exhausting, develop your own timeline and set the agenda. Perhaps a simpler way to capture the stories is a program called StoryWorth. The company sends your loved one a weekly prompt/question with an easy way to record their stories. At the end of the year, they receive a bound book of their memories.[14]

It is such a gift to subsequent generations to hear survivor stories of the Great Depression, the world wars, families that were torn apart because of poverty or prejudice, and the resilience of former generations. It's especially wonderful to hear a beloved person's voice. If you or a your loved one is beginning to decline and their memory is fading, now is the time. Don't put it off.

Video Memoirs

A legacy project is a video life review. Some hospitals and community centers sponsor their own programs through which a person can make an appointment and a film crew and interviewer arrive to ask a few basic questions of the interviewee and then allow them to elaborate. Some legacy projects allow people to tell their whole life story, others film just a segment. The joy of participating in a program such as this is loved ones can see and hear a family member or friend tell their stories in their own voice. This is a great way to hear what they want to tell their family and the world. It's often very revealing what people will say in front of a camera if their guard is down. If a subject feels comfortable, it can be amazing at what the storyteller comes up with. In the words of my friend, "just let the tape roll." If you don't have a local legacy project program, a family member can set up a tripod with a video camera or a smartphone. Encourage the subject to tell the story from their living room on a couch.

Now that you've had some time to sort out housing, care, and ways to tell your story, your family knows what you want. It's time to address the medical challenges ahead.

Talking about Health and Illness

Everyone knows they are going to die, but no one really believes it.

—Spaulding Gray

Though we tremble before uncertain futures, may we meet illness, death and diversity with strength. May we dance in the face of our fears.

—Gloria Anzaldúa

Frank

The plan was to go to the AAA league baseball game for the Memorial Day celebration. They were well armed with sunscreen, hats, and water, but what seemed like a fun day turned into a nightmare. About halfway through the game, Frank started to feel faint and wasn't able to stand up. Then he started to throw up. Startled, his wife quickly tried to hydrate him and get him into the shade, but he was very weak in the knees and unable to walk well, really struggling. After a few minutes in his new seat, he threw up again—this time doubled over in pain with a face as white as chalk. A friend alerted the security guard, who in turn checked in with the paramedics, who walked the stretcher and wheelchair up the 60 or so steps to where he was seated.

Frank was unable to answer all the questions they asked, so his wife feared cognitive impairment. The paramedics carried him out of the stadium to the emergency van parked outside, while his wife tried to compose herself and find their family to let them know what was happening. Then the wait. Nearly 30 minutes later, while they were re-routing him to a hospital nearer to their home, his wife exchanged keys with the family so the car would be taken to someone's home, and she took off to the Emergency Department (ED). More waiting, more uncertainty. Finally, the doctor assessed the situation and noted that dehydration and heat stroke were probably the cause. They would keep him under observation for seven hours and then decide whether to release him after the MRI and other scans were complete. Because Frank was under observation and in the hospital less than 24 hours, he was considered an ED patient and not admitted to a unit. He and his wife went home more exhausted than they had ever been due to sleep deprivation and all the questions swirling around in their heads. The result? They needed to change his medication and be more vigilant about hydration throughout the day. The bill? It was over $71,000, of which they paid approximately $2,000. They wondered what would have happened if they hadn't had insurance. And later they learned that all those tests may not have been necessary, but they were done and they had to be paid for by the patient or by the insurance company. What Frank and his wife learned that day was it is necessary to be vigilant about medical personnel intervention in a hospital, and that it is necessary to be your own advocate and express how you feel about the proposed procedure, test, or surgery.

Victoria

A newly minted executive at a technology firm, Victoria had worked her way up the food chain into one of the better cubicles. She even had a window! At 27, she'd saved up enough to buy a car and was excited to celebrate the weekend with friends after a big project at work was done. Sadly, on the ride home, she realized her friend at the wheel had partied a little too much. The car spun out of control on a remote highway and Victoria ended up at the bottom of a ravine with sirens blaring and light pointed at her pupils. After she was loaded on a gurney and whisked off to the emergency room, X-rays indicated Victoria's spinal cord was severed and she had lost the use of one of her legs.

Victoria's parents (including an absentee father who returned from Mexico after 15 years) and other relatives gathered for the family meeting that the hospital had set up. The medical team introduced themselves and explained their roles and the care that was planned for Victoria's transition to rehabilitation. Then they waited for a response. But no one seemed to be listening. The room was divided into two camps that were loudly debating their views. One group was insisting the doctors perform a miracle and get Victoria back to "her normal life," while the other group just wanted all the interventions to end and for the doctors to simply make Victoria "comfortable." Her mother clung to the bed and cried. Victoria's partner paced the room and remained silent. Her father argued for the better part of a half-hour with the medical team, informing them that they weren't doing all they could.

Victoria had had enough. Mustering her energy and courage, Victoria was ready to declare what *she* wanted. She was the one living in her body, not them. Yes, life was unfair, and yes, she was frustrated with the situation, but she let the medical team know what she was willing to do. The room went silent. Then one by one the faces in the room filled with tears. Finally, the attending doctor said, "Thank you, Victoria, we'll follow your wishes."

Your Chapter 3 Checklist:

1. Answer the "What Are My Goals of Care?" questionnaire and have a discussion about your goals of care with your medical team and the key support people in your life.

2. Learn about the roles of the various health care professionals.

3. Understand the patient advocate's job and know how and when to contact one.

4. Identify good candidates to be your health care proxies and fill out your durable power of attorney for health care,

advance directive/living will, HIPAA authorization form, and the Physician Order for Life Sustaining Treatment (POLST) form. Have the forms notarized and witnessed.

As chapter 2, "Making Wishes Known to Loved Ones," makes clear, many of us struggle to talk about the things that really matter in our lives. In fact, health and death are two topics that are out of bounds for many people even in close-knit families. And even when we or someone we love has a health problem or emergency, we may find ourselves unprepared to discuss the situation, the options, and our preferences.

This chapter is about talking about health issues and learning how to say what needs to be said for optimal outcomes and clear communication. In this chapter, I also discuss the paperwork you should fill out to make sure your wishes and needs about health care are communicated in a clear and legal manner. You will also learn about the people whom you meet in the health care system and how to negotiate with them to get the best possible care and to advocate for yourself and loved ones.

Defining, Understanding, and Discussing a Condition

Defining a medical condition is difficult. Few of us have the skill of the physician or surgeon to give detailed explanations of diagnoses (diseases, conditions, illnesses) and prognoses (likely outcomes with or without therapies). For a person with a diagnosis, talking about it requires they grasp and understand the medical information and it also involves emotional stamina; the pressure to learn all this comes at a time when you don't have a lot of extra energy. Medical practitioners are actively trying to do all they can to address your health care needs and develop a plan of care and you need to participate. It is stressful. Add the emotional stress of dealing with family members, relationships, and lost professional and personal dreams, and it can feel overwhelming to be discussing your condition and your options with people.

But a diagnosis can't be wished away. It is for you to own and decide how you want to manage it. Like Victoria, you may have to shout your "declaration of independence" as to what you are willing to do. You may know you have adenocarcinoma, but do you know what that really is, or your chance of survival? Do you know if there are other complications with the disease or with the therapies to cure it? Take the time to educate yourself. Ask your doctor for a detailed written definition and suggestions for resources you can explore. Get on the internet and search for articles written by doctors who are experts on your illness and who have spent years researching their respective fields. Learn about the research underway that might change the future for people with your diagnosis. Arm yourself with pages of questions that someone will have to answer before you are willing to sign a waiver for a procedure or surgery. Figure out your care goals and how you can meet them. One of the best ways to do this is to have a goals-of-care discussion, which I discuss in the next section of the chapter.

Discussing Goals of Care

Often, when we tackle a new program, we set goals for ourselves in order to establish what we want to achieve and set ourselves up to reach our objectives. A goals-of-care discussion accomplishes these same things. Perhaps you have a new diagnosis and you've done your research, talked to some other patients in a support group, and sat down with members of your family. In your initial conversations with doctors, they will want to know your wishes as the disease or illness progresses. You may have already expressed your general wishes in an advance directive (which I discuss in more detail in this chapter; see pages 77–80) but the goals-of-care questions I present in this section drill down a little deeper. When you meet with physicians and other health care folks, they come with their points to cover, you bring your questions, and somewhere in the middle of your conversation, a plan emerges on how to tackle your particular challenges.

The *"What Are My Goals of Care?"* questionnaire below features a list of sample questions for you to answer in preparation to meet with your health care team. You can find a blank copy of this questionnaire in worksheet form in the appendix on page 205 as well.

▬▬ Questionnaire: What Are My Goals of Care? ▬▬

1. What is my current understanding of where I am with my illness? (*What have you heard already from your health care team? What have you learned from the internet or friends and family? What is your current understanding of what is happening to your body?*)

2. What has the doctor communicated with me so far? (*Has the doctor actually shared a prognosis or what is likely to happen? Have they communicated the kind of therapeutic options that are part of their plan of care?*)

3. How much more information about my current condition and future prognosis would I like to have? What do I want to know? What do I need to know? (*In some cultures,*

*a patient is never told what is happening; information is
only shared with a point person, such as the eldest child in the
family, who then decides what the patient needs to know. What
are your cultural beliefs about knowing and sharing difficult
information?*)

4. What are my biggest fears and worries? (*Are you scared
   that you won't be able to care for others [children or a spouse]
   physically or financially? Are you scared to lose control? Are
   you frightened of being in pain or suffering physically? Are you
   worried about being a burden or lingering too long?*)

5. What gives me strength as I think about the future and my
   health concerns or illness? (*Is it your family or friends, faith
   or religion, a support group, or specific activities, like travel,
   reading, writing, gardening, or socializing with family and
   friends?*)

6. Which abilities are so critical to my life that I cannot
   imagine living without them? (*Is it being able to communicate
   with others? Are they walking, driving, and living at home
   alone? Is it taking care of your activities of daily living [ADLs]
   such as feeding, toileting, and dressing yourself?*)

7. If my health situation worsens, what's most important
   to me? (*Do you want to achieve an important life goal that
   you have not yet accomplished? Is it important for you to have
   mental awareness above all else? Do you want to do all you can
   to protect and support your family? Is it most important for you
   to be at home as long as possible, be physically comfortable as
   long as possible, or to be independent?*)

8. If I become sicker, how much am I willing to go through
   for the possibility of gaining more time? (*Do you want
   to avoid some procedures or treatments if their benefit is not*

substantial? Are you willing to be on a ventilator, live in a nursing home, endure physical discomfort or severe pain, spend time in the ICU, undergo invasive tests or procedures, or have a feeding tube?)

9. How much does my health care proxy/durable power of attorney agent (see pages 77–80) or family know about my wishes and priorities?

Armed with your answers from this questionnaire, you can have a goals-of-care discussion with your family and with your health care team. Communicating this information allows your medical team to understand your needs. And your primary physician will likely note your preferences in your permanent medical chart as well. Although this discussion doesn't take the place of legal documents, such as a durable power of attorney for health care or advance directive (which are covered later in this chapter on pages 77–80), it does create a roadmap. Your goals-of-care wishes are intimately linked to the legal documents discussed in this chapter. For example, if you have not filled out a durable power of attorney for health care or advance directive, you may want to take those form(s) with you as you work through the goals-of-care questions with your doctor.

Requesting a Timeline

As you probably know already, illness doesn't fit into a calendar very neatly. You can ask for a timeline from your medical team, but expect pushback. Setting a precise timeline is difficult. When you are seriously ill, your doctors will offer different therapies to see what works, and depending on your body's response to these therapies, they figure out their next steps. Then there will be times of evaluation and reporting back to let you know where you are. Still, it's okay to inform the medical team of your priorities and tell them about dates that matter such as a wedding date, an anniversary, an expected birth, or a graduation. They will try to work around those times.

The Health Care Cast of Characters

Who are the folks that you will you be talking to about your health care concerns? In the current medical universe, especially in a teaching hospital, you may have countless teams of specialists hovering over your bed or participating in and observing your procedures. As you likely already know, your primary physician is the person responsible to assign specialists for your comprehensive care, but the following is a cast of additional characters who may march across your stage:

- *Doctors.* Medical doctors (also called physicians) are the experts who probe how you are doing physically or medically or psychologically. Their decade (or longer) of graduate education is generally the longest of all the medical personnel. Most doctors have additional specialty expertise in an area such as family health, cardiology (heart), neurology (brain), hepatology (liver), pulmonology (lung), dermatology (skin), oncology (cancer), psychology or psychiatry (behavior and mental health), or a myriad of other specialties. Typically, a doctor works with a team based on his or her own specialty. Be aware that multiple teams will roam through your hospital room, looking for clues as to how they can intervene in your care. The work of these additional team members will also be reflected in your billing from the hospital.

■ *Hospitalists.* Hospitalists are physicians that coordinate the care of patients' in a hospital. They are the "captains of the ships," organizing the communication between different doctors who care for a patient by serving as the point of contact for other doctors and nurses for questions and updates, and delineating a comprehensive plan of care. They are also the main physician for family members to contact for updates on a loved one.

■ *Physician Assistants, Advanced Practice Providers, Nurse Practitioners, Advanced Practitioners.* These core staff members handle the majority of most common ailments in a busy multi-faceted hospital. They tend to be responsible for annual exams, express or urgent care, and some areas of the Emergency Department. They are licensed to prescribe medication, can declare a person's death, and often are trained in specialties just as doctors are. Although not as extensively educated as an MD, their skills are invaluable to doctors, who rely on these highly skilled associates in clinics and on hospital units.

■ *Registered Nurses (RNs).* Registered nurses are the hands-on practitioners who are assigned to specific patients. Unlike most doctors, who work on multiple units and patients depending on their team assignment or expertise, nurses are on a dedicated floors with patients as a primary focus. Nurses often work as team coordinators with medical assistants or LPNs to manage day-to-day routine care. They also work with the doctor regarding symptomatic, emergent issues.

■ *Licensed Practical Nurses (LPNs).* LPNs assist with the hands-on work of medication, toileting, walking, taking vitals, and dressing in a care facility. LPNs are common in nursing homes and long-term care units. An LPN can answer questions regarding medications, arrange for a patient to take a walk, help ordering from the kitchen, and make sure a bed gets changed. A patient can generally request anything from an LPN that a nurse or doctor isn't assigned to handle. Like the rest of the medical team, LPNs document their work in the chart notes.

- *Medical Assistants.* A medical assistant performs administrative duties: updates and files medical records, fills out insurance forms, handles correspondence, schedules appointments, arranges for hospital admission and laboratory services, and does billing and bookkeeping.

- *Case Managers/Discharge Planners.* These are perhaps the most overworked and underappreciated group of personnel in a hospital. Case managers and discharge planners oversee all patient care and discharges based on insurance parameters. They arrange for family meetings, aftercare, and rehabilitation, provide community resources, and educate family on what to expect once the patient is back home. If you need suggestions for caregivers, rehab centers, financial aid resources, home resources, and transportation, this is the person you seek. They also provide education on how to dress a wound, handle home care, and locate additional counselors.

- *Social Workers.* The role of the social worker has changed dramatically in the past few decades. Previously their role was to handle family dynamics and emotional issues, in-home support, and social, housing, transportation, and financial concerns. Now, most social workers are licensed clinical social workers (LCSWs) or licensed counselors who are adept at skills as diverse as psychiatric counseling, mindfulness and meditation coaching, and negotiating and facilitating family meetings. It's not unusual to have a social worker interfacing for patient in-home support services with the county, working on social security payments with the federal government, handling disability issues with the state government agencies, and finding or providing counseling for grieving children or family members. The complex variety of psychosocial issues has expanded the job description of social worker to a much wider universe.

▪ *Radiologists.* Radiologists are medical doctors who specialize in making diagnoses from images. Plain films (X-ray images of a body part, taken from anterior, posterior, lateral, or oblique projections) or regular X-rays are the simplest forms of imaging, but now CT scans (computed tomography scans that result in cross-sectional imaging of the body), MRIs (magnetic resonance imaging, which use magnetism to form images), and ultrasounds (which generate images using sound waves) are widely used. Radiologists further specialize in areas such as breast imaging, neuroimaging of the brain and nervous system, and musculoskeletal imaging. The subspecialty of interventional radiology includes both diagnosis and treatment of certain conditions. Nuclear medicine (which is sometimes part of a radiology department and sometimes a separate department) similarly involves both diagnosis and certain therapies. Radiologists work closely with referring physicians, such as oncologists, to assess and help manage patients.

- *Psychological Counselors.* Sometimes just being in a hospital can precipitate a mental crisis, especially if a diagnosis or prognosis is sudden and/or negative. For patients who are struggling with emotional or sexual assault, loss and grief, or horrific news, or if they are struggling to cope for any reason, a hospital employs its own staff of psychological and psychiatric doctors to assess and assist. If a patient is hospitalized, being able to see someone about psychological concerns "in house" can be a blessing and may facilitate scheduling subsequent visits after a hospital stay is over.

- *Chaplains.* A chaplain is unique in that a patient doesn't have to see a chaplain as part of a treatment regime. However, a chaplain's role is essential. Many churches have shrinking congregations and are closing their doors, and many people have turned away from established churches, temples, or mosques. Yet those who have embedded faith or spirituality from their childhood may still be searching for answers to the meaning and purpose of their life, especially as they face mortality. Many people are trying to reconnect with a place of worship and seek support. Often patients and their families find themselves asking questions about a higher power, and existential questions such as, Why is this happening? and, Why is this happening to me? Patients may be fearful of death and worried that they will not have enough time to complete things or to thank or forgive the people that have altered their lives. Interfaith chaplains are trained to handle all of these situations as well as connect people to their faith of origin or rituals that can bring meaning and comfort to a hospital room. Handling baptisms, weddings, memorials, prayers, meditations, drum circles, and countless other rituals and programs, chaplains straddle the diverse worlds of metaphysical, existential, and esoteric matters.

- *Respiratory Therapists.* These technicians handle anything related to the lungs including respiration, intubation/extubation, CPAP (continuous positive airway pressure is the leading therapy for sleep apnea), breathing exercises, techniques, or machines to enhance the breathing process such as ventilators. Respiratory therapists are also part of the stroke/rapid response teams for trauma patients because lung functioning and oxygen supply are essential to maintaining brain health.

- *Speech Therapists.* These professionals are more than diction coaches or facilitators who train patients to speak after a stroke. They understand all the functions of the throat and swallowing and the delicate processes of vocal cords. They help with exercises that facilitate timbre and pitch in a voice and communication for patients who have lost the capacity to speak.

- *Physical Therapists.* PTs handle patients ambulatory and rehabilitation processes and are in charge of reconditioning muscular and skeletal parts of the body. For instance, if you've been in an accident and your muscles, joints, and bones have been disrupted, fractured, or broken, this person is in charge of creating a plan of care for you to stand, walk, and strengthen your body in order for you to function again. Some of this work is done in the hospital, but the majority is done in rehabilitation/subacute centers and clinics where therapists schedule frequent appointments to help patients regain as much physical independence as they possibly can.

- *Occupational Therapists.* OTs help patients regain the basic skills of life. Their work can range from assisting recovery from brain injury to end-of-life care. Along with PTs, they help people adjust to living with a new normal in terms of physical limitations and functions. Like PTs, OTs provide one-on-one therapy to achieve personal goals, such as cooking a meal, gardening, or working on a specific project. For example, if you want to return to an educational setting to finish a degree, the OT can create a plan for accommodations for driving or using machinery, for instance, to make your goals a reality. Occupational therapists also run therapeutic groups, work in collaboration with clinical psychologists and case managers, lead public workshops, and generally provide assistance in training for their patients to live as independently as possible.

- *Dietitians (or Dieticians).* An expert in human nutrition, a dietitian alters nutrition based on medical conditions and individual needs. Dietitians are regulated health care professionals licensed to assess, diagnose, and treat nutritional problems. An RD (registered dietitian) or RDN (registered dietitian nutritionist) must participate in internships and take a national exam. They hold graduate degrees with specialties in sports, pediatrics, renal (kidney), oncological (cancer), or gerontological (older adults) nutrition or food allergies. Like other practitioners, dietitians help set goals and prioritize.

- *Phlebotomists.* A phlebotomist draws blood samples from patients or donors and prepares those samples for medical testing. Analyzed in a clinical laboratory, the blood samples are used to diagnose illness, evaluate the effectiveness of medications, and determine whether a patient is receiving proper nutrition. In the hospital, it may be necessary to have multiple blood draws in one day due to the needs of the various medical teams or to test the progress of various therapies.

■ *Financial Assistants.* Hospitals have people to counsel patients in financial matters, especially when people are inadequately insured or unable to pay. Personnel in this department assist people in understanding insurance coverage, indicate what is covered and not covered, and assist in developing payment plans. Like any other business, hospitals want to be reimbursed the full amount of their bill, so they are willing to work on creative solutions to get debts paid. In the event patients are disabled, unemployed, or simply unable to pay due to lack of resources, some hospitals may negotiate bills to an affordable amount or forgive *portions of it through a benevolence fund. This is a rare solution.*

■ *Hospital Ombudsperson/Patient Advocate.* An ombudsperson's or patient advocate's job is to listen to your grievance and make suggestions to address your concerns, find a solution, or mediate an additional meeting with appropriate hospital personnel to resolve the issue.

Medical Bills and Your Responsibilities

You may find yourself facing financial hardship when you face a serious medical issue. In a recent academic research study, 66.5% of all bankruptcies in the US were tied to medical expenses either due to the high cost of care or due to lost wages resulting from time off from work.[15] This statistic is all the more reason to know what a hospital is proposing as a plan of care and how the care will be billed. Never sign a waiver or an authorization form unless you know what the care you are agreeing to will cost and who is paying for it.

Train the people who are your advance directive agents to get to know the hospital personnel that are assigned to your case and engage in dialogue with them about finances as well as care issues. If you do not pay a bill and fail to communicate with the finance department about that bill, the hospital generally assigns bill collection to a collection agency, and then no one wins. The hospital gets a fraction of what you are paying, and the collection agency can make your life miserable. Know what part of the bill you are responsible for so you or your power of attorney or agent can fight your case.

Advocating in the Hospital: Standing Up for Yourself

Finding Your Voice (More from Frank's Wife)

I can remember how helpless I felt when Frank had his Memorial Day incident. In just 20 hours, we were taken in an ambulance to the Emergency Department, then on to an "observation room," which was a pre-admission six-by-nine-foot space that contained both his bed and the chair I was given to sleep in. We encountered a cardiovascular

team, a neurological team, a hospitalist, three phlebotomists, a cleaning person, two shifts of nurses, three medical assistants, a dietician, two transport people, two MRI
technicians, a patient admission administrator, a social
worker, and a chaplain.

We also encountered too many clipboards to count,
filled with paperwork and official documents, all waiting
for signatures. Sleep deprived, I would have signed anything to get Frank out of there. To be fair, the hospital was
doing all they could to find the best solution for his emergency. But three blood tests in a span of five hours in the
middle of the night was over the top. Each medical team
wanted their own results. If I had had I my wits about me,
I would have said stop at one test and told everyone to
share the results in their charts.

As this story illustrates, it is important to know that as an
advocate for yourself or for your loved one, you have the right to
say no or to at least question why any procedure is being done.
Many people avoid confronting the experts because they think
the health care workers have knowledge and power on their side
and the patients and their families are therefore at their mercy.
People also assume doctors always know what to do, and that
may be the case. However, they don't know you or the patient
as well as you do. If you feel that they've gone one test too far,
speak up. If you feel the plan of care doesn't match what you
agreed to, speak up. Be clear with what you will tolerate, what
you are willing to pay for (especially if there is pushback from
your insurance company), and what your body or emotional
state can handle. Sometimes speaking up and asking why is all
it takes to get a second opinion or a frank discussion.

But what if you or the patient you are advocating for isn't being heard? Or a procedure was handled poorly or one you didn't authorize was done anyway? Or you may feel that differences of opinion are holding up care or one medical team is not communicating with another. In these situations, you can bump up your grievance to higher authority. In situations such as these, you should feel free to contact a hospital ombudsperson, sometimes known as a patient advocate (see the list of hospital personnel on page 71). Hospitals and clinics loathe malpractice suits, so this group of professionals is key in avoiding legal problems. Take the time to reach these people if you feel like you can't resolve the issue on your own.

Special Advocates: HICAP

The Health Insurance Counseling and Advocacy Program (HICAP) is a free and objective counseling program that helps inform people about Medicare. Volunteer counselors are trained to help patients understand their specific rights and health care options. HICAP also offers free educational programs to groups of Medicare beneficiaries, their families, or providers on a variety of Medicare and other health insurance–related topics. These topics include prescription drugs, help for low-income households, Medigap, Medicare advantage programs, health insurance options, appeals, billing and claims, disabilities, long-term care, health care reform, and fraud and abuse. Even if you don't think or aren't sure if you need this advice, you may want to sign up for HICAP. There may be a program, additional income source, or deadline you need to address. My spouse and I spent the better part of three months trying to straighten out a misunderstanding with our insurance coverage when I was working as an independent contractor. Had we taken the time to access HICAP resources to plan our transition to Medicare coverage, we could have saved countless hours and stress.

Your Health Care Documents and Advocates

Now that you have thought more about your goals of care and you know more about the health care team, you are ready to record your wishes in writing in health care documents and choose and assign your advocates. Every adult should have an advance directive to explain the type of health care they do or do not want when they can't make their own decisions. Every adult should also appoint someone who can speak for them to make sure their wishes are carried out. The fifty states have different forms for legal documents such as living wills and other legal health care documents. And to make things even more confusing, states use different terms to describe these forms. Here I try to summarize some general information about these health care forms. I begin with the most important document, the durable power of attorney for health care and advance directive.

What's in a Name?

In this book you will see references to any or all of the following terms when I speak of the people who help carry out your wishes after your demise (note that the term "decedent" refers to the person who has died):

- *Personal Representative/Successor Trustee/Executor.* Most people designate a personal representative in their will (an "executor") and/or trust (a "successor trustee"). This person is empowered to make decisions regarding finances and property, and administer the estate after your death, based on your written wishes included in the document. This person does not have the ability to change your instructions or make decisions that would be contrary to your specific instructions. A personal representative is the broader term that encompasses both the term executor and successor trustee.

- *Agent.* A person who is assigned by a legal document to make decisions for you if you are unable. An agent under a durable financial power of attorney is the person who will handle specific financial decisions and issues on your behalf should you become incapacitated. An agent can be the same individual you name as a trustee, an executor, or a health care proxy (see below).

- *Proxy.* A health care proxy has the legal authority to make medical decisions for you.

- *Power of Attorney.* A power of attorney is the document used to give someone authority to make financial decisions in your stead. So, while a proxy may choose a retirement community for you if preauthorized to do so by you, it is your agent under your power of attorney who releases the funds to pay for it.

    Some people end up choosing the same person for all of the roles listed here. It all depends on the dynamics of family and your circumstances. It's typically required that you also name a second/alternative person or even a third in case the first person can't serve in the role.

Your nominees act for you in sickness and after death, so be sure to choose someone steady, trustworthy, patient, and detail oriented. Choose someone who has your and your family's best wishes at heart. Make sure they are someone you feel can carry out the responsibilities listed in the checklist on pages 148–151 in chapter 6, "Figuring Out What Happens Next," and make sure they understand that checklist and what you are asking them to do.

Durable Power of Attorney for Health Care and Advance Directive (Living Will)

A power of attorney (POA) is written authorization to represent or act on someone else behalf. A financial power of attorney deals with the financial and legal matters. A durable power of attorney for health care names someone to communicate your health care wishes and end-of-life treatment instructions. In some states, a durable power of attorney for health care is different from an advance directive but in some states they are combined in one document. An advance directive (also called a living will) specifies the treatment you want if you are at the end of your life and can no longer communicate. So while an advance directive/living will makes your wishes known in a written statement, in a living will you do not have to appoint a person to act on your behalf and make those decisions. A durable power of attorney for health care specifically does that. However, some advance directive forms also allow you to appoint a proxy. In short, the durable power of attorney for health care is the permission slip you give to someone to handle your medical affairs when you can no longer speak for yourself and the advance directive says what your medical care preferences are. The various forms of these two basic documents officially and legally confirm a patient's wishes. You can find links to these forms on pages 199–200.

Most hospitals, clinics, and state governments are happy to provide you free forms to fill out for yourself or loved ones. You can also find these forms on line. If you use a form from your health care provider or one you find on line, you may be able to save attorney fees. These two key documents—durable power of attorney for health care and advance directive in their variable forms and iterations—address four basic issues, which I discuss in the content that follows.

The first issue, covered legally by the durable power of attorney for health care, is naming your agent or proxy person(s). If you are incapacitated, your health care proxy makes sure your medical decisions are honored and your wishes are carried out. It is especially important to have a health care proxy if you and your family potentially disagree about health care and treatment.

When you ask someone to be your agent or proxy, you may want to share with them the list in chapter 6, "Figuring Out What Happens Next," that details their responsibilities after your death. You can find a checklist on pages 148–151. This is not a casual ask, and they and you should know what you are asking them to do.

As you look for an agent or proxy, find someone who knows you, your wishes, and how you wish to be cared for during an emergency or end of life. They should also know their way around a hospital. And be sure to list more than one person. If they cannot reach the first person on your list, your medical team will automatically call the second, then the third, and then on to other family members. Remember to also list those who you *don't want* to be contacted (for example, a former spouse or an estranged member of your family).

The second set of topics, typically covered in both the advance directive and the durable power of attorney for health care, are your preferences for specific life-saving interventions and in what situation interventions are to be made (usually in an emergency or at the end of life). Do you want chest compressions, ventilators, feeding tubes, dialysis, or simple pain meds and sleep? This section allows you to be very specific and add personal notes. The answers you list in the "What Are My Goals of Care?" questionnaire on page 61 can provide the foundation for your advance directive.

The third issue these key legal documents can address is organ donation. Many people sign up for organ donation through the Department of Motor Vehicles and then forget to tell someone, or they do not have their license with them when an emergency occurs. You can choose to give an organ donor network permission to assess your organs for a transplant. It does not guarantee you will be a donor.

The fourth important element of these documents is contact information for your primary care physician and/or specialists who know your medical history.

Some of the health care power of attorney and advance directive forms are available online to download and fill in, such as *Five Wishes*[16] (which is honored in 42 states). They have a narrative tone and address more detailed and personalized questions including what kind of rituals, prayers, and people would you like to have at the end of life. Other advance directives ask "meaning and purpose" questions to assist the physician in determining what matters to you and if there are milestones in your life that need to be addressed. Again, your filled-out "What are

My Goals of Care?" questionnaire on page 61 can help you as you make the choices expressed in your advance directive.

Once you have filled out your key legal documents, you sign them as required by your state law. Most documents will specifically state whether they require them to be signed in front of a notary or can be signed in front of two witnesses. If signed in front of two witnesses, most states require that only one of the witnesses can be a family member and neither signatory can be one of the people named as an agent in the documents. Once the document has been properly executed, you need to send a copy to the medical records department at your hospital, one to your clinic or doctor, and a copy to each of your agents. You should keep the original in a safe place.

Organ/Body Donation

If you have already filled out an advance directive, your wishes about organ donation may be included. However, with most hospitals, whole body donation will also require a separate application. Although it is altruistic to declare that a body will be given to scientific research at time of death, not everyone will qualify, and you need to be granted permission to do so. Take the time, while you are filling out your advance directive, to decide whether or not you wish to donate your whole body, and if you do, fill out any additional forms that are needed. They are available at your hospital or medical school. Inform your family and agents of your wishes and give everyone a copy. Please keep in mind, many hospitals and medical schools do not return the remains of the person after they have done their research. Be sure to read the fine print for the agency's specific regulations.

HIPAA Authorization Form and Physician Orders for Life-Sustaining Treatment (POLST)

Often the advance directive for health care, durable power of attorney, HIPAA authorization for release of health information form, and POLST are grouped together as they together represent your medical wishes. HIPAA (Health Insurance Portability and Accountability Act) is the law that protects your medical privacy. In the event of an emergency, you may want to authorize an individual to receive your medical information so they can be apprised of the situation. A HIPAA authorization form allows the person you designate to be contacted and get involved. A link for a HIPAA authorization form for any state is listed in the back of this book, on page 200.

A Physician Orders for Life Saving Treatment form or *POLST* is a bright pink form that you fill out and then must be signed by a doctor. This form tells the EMT (emergency medical technician) personnel, skilled nursing/assisted living facilities, or any other life-saving teams your preferences if you need emergency treatment. A common example situation might be when a neighbor calls 911 after someone falls. When the ambulance arrives, the POLST form, displayed in a prominent place, informs the EMTs what kind of life-saving procedures can or cannot be carried out. Your POLST should be on your refrigerator or in plain sight. Although many people display it on their refrigerators, other people even keep this on their person or in the glove box of their car. You can find links to these forms on pages 199–200.

Once you have appointed your proxy and expressed your preferences in writing, what happens when a situation arises and these preferences need to be addressed? In the rest of the book, I discuss just that.

Now that you've thought more about how you want to be treated in the medical setting and established the paperwork to make that happen, it's time to put your financial and legal house in order. I discuss how to do that in detail in the following chapter.

4

Putting Your House in Order

You can't go back and change the beginning, but you can start where you are and change the ending.

—C. S. Lewis

Set your house in order, . . . you shall not recover.

—2 Kings 20:1b

Lucille

Lucille died at 67. She had a tumor in her brain and died after numerous chemo and radiation treatments. She was survived by an assortment of children from her deceased husband's first marriage, her first marriage, and grandchildren from both sides. Lucille's death occurred in the hospital after a protracted and lengthy stay filled with hospitalists, specialists, and her primary doctor. All of these medical personnel were left to ponder the best plan of care and determine what should be done because Lucille refused to sign an advance directive. Her children, unaware of her wishes, allowed whatever recommended tests to be carried out on her. Because the tests were doctor endorsed, her family assumed the tests would prolong her life indefinitely. They didn't.

At the church for the memorial planning, the family spent most of their time arguing about money and who should be invited to the ceremony. No one had any clue about Lucille's wishes for a send-off or what was to be said or sung. The pastor acted as ringleader while the family processed their anger and grief and argued over the inheritance. Back at the house, the treasure hunt was underway, with the invited children combing the rooms for clues as to where the estate summary might be found, with dreams of sugar plums and new cars dancing in their heads. Meanwhile, those who were not invited for the excavation considered hiring a lawyer to make sure they "got their fair share."

But there were no documents to discover as Lucille had never prepared nor collected them. And what Lucille's survivors also didn't anticipate was the enormous bill that awaited them from the hospital. They forgot to account for that and the final taxes and estate costs while they were mentally adding up their inheritances. Two years later, with attorney fees mounting, the estate was still not settled due to a lack of a will and of money to pay probate costs. Lucille died intestate (without a will in place) and the state had its own formula for redistribution of the remaining monies. The two sides of the family are still not speaking to one another.

Ollie

In sharp contrast to Lucille, Ollie had known that planning ahead was wise. A career military person, he decided early on what he needed to set in place before his death. Although he was estranged from one of his two daughters, he opted to treat both daughters equally so his wife would not have to argue or settle any costly legal disputes. He had a durable power of attorney for health care and an advance directive (see chapter 3, "Talking about Health and Illness") signed and in place specifying his wishes and concerns. His trust and will were also up to date. He had updated all his financial accounts and insurance policies and shared his account numbers for his pension and Social Security. He made a list of his personal PINs, codes, and passwords, as well as a list of all other confidential information that he shared only with his wife so she could safely keep it and then easily access the information upon his death. He also had a list of his contacts at the VA and other advisors and resource people in his life. He had preplanned (not prepaid) his burial and his memorial service—the scriptures, songs, and the message he wanted to have read. He had made an inventory of possessions he wanted to pass on to his two daughters and had written a loving letter of memory and thanks to his wife, children, and close family members. Once he had prepared and collected all this crucial information, Ollie had placed it all in a white binder. The information in the binder was tabbed and indexed and ready for review. His wife, children, attorney, advisors, and pastor each were given their own copy of the binder. After this was done, Ollie could live the rest of his life in peace.

When he died, it was a joyous, celebratory end; there was no treasure hunt, no arguments—just thanksgiving.

Your Chapter 4 Checklist:

1. Learn the importance of creating a personal archive or binder of essential information and documents for your heirs.

2. Begin to assemble the relevant information and documents you need to create your own personal archive.

3. Contact the professionals who can help you complete your archive.

The stories of Lucille and Ollie illustrate the importance of taking the time to put your house in order and then getting on with your life. You can make the choice to be like Ollie or to be like Lucille, and making the right choice can save your survivors endless sadness, confusion, and anxiety.

Preventing the Treasure Hunt: Ensuring Your Heirs Know Your Wishes

At this point, you may be ready to put this book down and take a break. Few people look forward to financial or legal decision-making and planning. But taking care of financial and legal matters is necessary, and a bit of planning now may save you or your heir's hundreds, perhaps even thousands, of dollars in taxes and unnecessary legal fees. That fact alone hopefully might make you feel more motivated, and it might not be as difficult as you think. It's likely you already have some of the important forms filled out and the information you need to set your house in order at hand. And if not, I hope this chapter encourages you to get organized so that your family can avoid the treasure hunt for documents that should be easy to access.

Many people work countless years building up assets, a portfolio, or an estate. It would be tragic to have that inventory end up in court with the legal fees mounting daily and no end in sight because the proper documents and files were not prepared and/or family can't find the files. There are countless high-profile stories about unsettled estates, like those of Howard Hughes, Aretha Franklin, or Prince, that should inspire you to avoid such issues for your heirs.

Creating an Archive of Financial and Legal Information for Survivors

This chapter is an annotated detailed inventory of the documents you need to collect and share to educate your heirs about your assets and your debts. Documents on this list also indicate how to proceed with medical, financial, and general matters when you can no longer speak for yourself. It may take time to collect all this information in one place, but it's worth the effort.

You may have already begun to think about the documents you might gather together in a binder to help your survivors easily sort out the final paperwork after your death. For some, a binder may seem a little outdated, but it's a good place to start the discussion about the documents you can prepare and gather before death. Unless you've gone completely paperless, most of your documents may be initially on paper anyway, so collecting these paper documents is a good way to begin. You can scan your hard copies and create digital files later.

Many banks and financial institutions have their own inventory fill-in-the-blank paper or online forms. There are also general resources such as Mint from Intuit (mint.com), a free, web-based personal financial management service for the US and Canada, and other online and digital programs. There are also spiral notebooks—such as *Final Wishes* by Patty Moorhead and *I'm Dead, Now What? Important Information about My Belongings, Business Affairs, and Wishes* published by Peter Pauper Press and *When I'm Gone: My Info, Wishes, and Thoughts* by Journals Unlimited—that are designed to help summarize and categorize data. There is also a digital program called Canopy that will help you store and lock down your information in the cloud (data storage that is accessed through the internet.) It is your call on which of these resources will be more useful to you and all these are listed in the resources in the appendix.

Another Bit of Advice

While snail mail is more and more a thing of the past, encourage your heirs to tend to your mailbox after your death. All sorts of financial and legal information may arrive at your home and clog the mailbox and create a temptation for a criminal. Ask your executor or personal representative to have the post office stop your mail and go through whatever is collected with an eye for financial and legal documents.

Collecting Essential Information and Documents

The following content details the essential information and documents you will want to collect to have in your personal archive to share with your heirs and the people who will help your heirs when you die. You can find this list in the nearby box and also in the appendix.

Checklist of Essential Information and Documents

This list is the same one used to organize the chapter content that follows. You can use the following list as a table of contents for your own binder or online archive of information:

I. Financial Information

Inventory of Assets and Liabilities

Insurance Policies: Life, Long-Term Care, Auto, and Homeowners

Additional Income Sources: Social Security, Pension Plans, Wages, and Employment Accounts

Retirement Plans

Individual Retirement Accounts (IRAs) and Roth IRAs

After-Death Arrangements: Burial, Cremation, Memorial and Funeral Rites, Organ Donation, Ecoburial, etc.

Outstanding Debts and Regular Ongoing Bills

Tax Documents

II. Legal and Estate Information

The Will

Trust Documents

Durable Power of Attorney (POA) for Finances

Durable Power of Attorney (POA) for Health Care, Advance Directive for Health Care, HIPAA authorization, and POLST

III. **Other Information**
      Military Service Information
      Personal Wishes and Gifts
      Pets

IV. **Original Documents**

V. **User ID, Passwords, PINs, Codes, etc.***

      * KEEP THIS INFORMATION IN A SEPARATE PLACE

Financial Information

My list of essential documents and information is divided into financial information and legal and estate matters. First, I address the key financial information.

Inventory of Assets and Liabilities

Your inventory of assets and liabilities is simply a list of what you own and what you owe. For example, you may have statements from your bank, receive updates from your stock and bond broker, or mutual fund manager and other institutions. Some people have a financial advisor who creates a spreadsheet and hands them a monthly and year-end report. That's a start. Add to these lists your home and vacation or rental properties, car(s), any private investments or limited partnerships, stock options, real estate investment trusts, Bitcoin/cyber currencies, and collectibles. In addition to listing your assets, you want to list your bank and savings account numbers and where your PINs and passcodes are located. This list of assets complete with account numbers and location will serve as a basis for any estate tax or capital gains that may need to be calculated at the time of your death. Along with assets such as these, you also need to consider any insurance policies you have.

Insurance Policies: Life, Long-Term Care, Auto, and Homeowners/Renters

Life Insurance.

Some life insurance policies include a cash-provision payout at the time of death, a savings account, or securities. Other policies contain special clauses that allow for premiums to be paid when you are unable to do so. Gather your life insurance policies and check the "face sheet" or insurance declaration page that lists the premium and payout provisions at death. Insurance payments are often distributed according to beneficiary designations kept with the account custodian. You must contact these other organizations to ensure all assets pass according to your wishes. Let heirs know the details of policies, policy numbers, and how to contact your insurance agent upon your death. List the agent who sold you the policy and their contact information if possible.

Long-Term Care Insurance.

Long-term care insurance policies can be a blessing if a person is confronted with long-term or terminal illness. These policies provide daily financial assistance with the cost of home care in both a person's own home or in assisted living and nursing facilities. Medicare does not provide this sort of assistance. As you can imagine, this can be a huge help. These policies, however, are often very costly or even unavailable due to the rising costs of care. If you have long-term care insurance, be sure to let your heirs know the policy deductible (the finances you are responsible for), the waiting period for benefits to begin, and the cost or premium. List the agent who sold you the policy and their contact information if possible. A post-death claim on this policy is a potentially huge blessing when there are outstanding health care bills at the time of death.

Auto Insurance.

Information on your auto insurance should be easy to collect as you probably pay either monthly or semiannually. Your heirs need to know the cost of the premium, what the deductible is, and the maximum payout for each car. List the agent who sold the policy and their contact information so your heirs can terminate or transfer the policy to new owners or recipients. Include a copy of your car registration; be sure to keep the pink slip (certificate of title) in your safety deposit box. (I discuss safety deposit box information later in this chapter on pages 110–111.)

Homeowners/Renters Insurance.

Check your policy fact sheet that covers all the particulars of what is covered, the deductible (the finances you are responsible for), the maximum payout, and the cost to maintain the policy after your death until the home or rental property is transferred, sold, or vacated. This information, as well the name of the agent who sold you the policy and their contact information, should be included in your financial document information archive contents. With a homeowners policy, you are protecting both the dwelling and the contents. With a renters policy, only the contents are covered and there is defined liability coverage if there is damage.

Additional Income Sources: Social Security, Pension Plans, Wages, and Employment Accounts

At the time of death, income may be rolling into your bank account from various sources. Social Security, pension institutions, and banks need to be notified when you die. There are countless stories about the Social Security Administration not finding out that a person has died, and their heirs continue to collect checks for months. This is fraud, and no one wants their heirs to be accused of fraud. For each of your income sources, list the name of the organization or company and a possible contact name and number and the monthly or annual amount of income this source provides. This is especially important for pension plans, as many plans have an annuity payout provision that pays a specific amount while you are alive and a second amount (usually reduced) to a beneficiary after your death.

If you are still being paid a set bi-weekly or monthly amount by your employer before your death, someone will need to contact your current employer or human resources department to inform them of your death. If you have a contact in human resources, include that name and phone number in your planning notebook. When heirs contact an employer, there may be other accounts to settle. Paid time off (PTO) accounts are common, as are health savings accounts (HSAs). PTO is accumulated time off work that must be used within a certain time period. A PTO account is generally cashed out at termination of employment. A health savings account is a type of savings account that lets you set aside money on a pretax basis to pay for qualified medical expenses. When an employed person dies, there may be balances in both PTO and HSA accounts. Your heirs may be able to apply those funds to the final bills from a hospital or clinic. The executor or personal representative needs to collect the information and make a claim to gain access to any credit or unpaid amounts that might exist. Any information you can provide them about these accounts will be helpful.

Retirement Plans

Another source of income is a retirement plan paid directly from your employer or a designated trustee. In your archive, list any relevant account numbers, the name of the employer/company, the amount paid to your bank or the amount you receive in the form of a check, and the frequency of payments along with the contact information. (Be sure to also list all your PINs and passwords, but keep these all in a separate place and do not share these with multiple people.) An instrument called a defined benefit plan is a common example of an employer-sponsored retirement plan. In a defined benefit plan, benefits are computed taking into account several factors, such as length of employment and salary history. 401(k), 403(b), and 457(b) plans are deferred compensation plans that allow an employee to divert a portion of their salary into long-term investments while lowering current taxable income.

Individual Retirement Accounts (IRAs) and Roth IRAs

An individual retirement account (IRA) is a tax-advantaged investing tool that individuals use to earmark funds for retirement savings. Depending on the individual's employment status, IRAs can be of various types and have different tax liabilities. Payouts for individual retirement accounts and Roth IRA accounts (which have different tax implications) are generally sent directly to your home and you are updated monthly, quarterly, and annually on earnings and payouts. Note that for some people these accounts are rolled into other larger accounts managed by financial planners and may be part of a larger portfolio, so check account numbers for duplicates.

In your archive, list any relevant account numbers, the name of the account holder, the amount paid to your bank or the amount you receive in the form of a check, and the frequency of payments along with the account contact information. (Also list all your user IDs, PINs, and passwords, but keep these all in a separate place and do not share these with multiple people.) Be sure to officially select the beneficiaries (the people who will receive the funds when you die). It's really discouraging when a person forgets to cancel a former spouse as a beneficiary of the account and heirs must scramble to attempt to correct the error.

After-Death Arrangements: Burial, Cremation, Ecoburial, Organ Donation, and Memorial and Funeral Rites

Designate specifics about your memorial and the way you want your body to be taken care of after death and prevent your family from having to deal with these decisions by making your plans and letting your heirs know what you have decided. Planning for a memorial in advance and discussing body disposition and rituals and ceremonies can be very helpful for family members. I have yet to hear from any family who loved planning a burial or a memorial. No one wants to think of themselves or a loved one six feet under. However, it never hurts to get at least an idea of what you or a loved one wants in order to avoid problems such as cultural faux pas or family arguments.

Make sure to communicate any strong desires so your family can carry out your wishes. This information should be part of your binder and part of your discussions with loved ones. Take the time to fill out both the "Body Disposition and Memorial Planning Worksheet" and "Eulogy and Obituary Planning Worksheet" in the appendix on pages 209–220 and add them to your archive. You can also read more about these topics in chapter 6, "Figuring Out What Happens Next," on pages 152–165.

Some people decide to prepay for disposition and memorial arrangements. If you make these types of arrangements, your archive is the place to include the contract for these services as well as details about what was paid for and what has been prearranged. (A good option is to preplan for disposition but not prepay unless you want to reserve a burial site and spaces are filling up near your family's area at the cemetery. Prepaid plans from a memorial franchise may work in one state but not transfer to another state.) Finances to pay for these plans can be kept in a separate account or be paid from an insurance trust policy. Just be sure to communicate their location with the people who will be making the arrangements.

If you have made provisions to donate your body to a medical school or institution, add the application and certification papers in this section of your archive. These plans are also best discussed with the family in person before your death if possible. Family needs to know your wishes in advance so they don't find out your wishes after your body is already in the ground or cremated and your ashes have been scattered at your favorite beach.

In addition to filling out the Body Disposition and Memorial Planning Worksheet in the appendix, consider writing an inventory of things to tell your family about how you want your death to be commemorated. Information can be as simple as a song list, a few poems or passages from favorite writers, scripture, a request for a certain person to speak, some final words, and a brief autobiography that can form the basis for a eulogy or obituary. Read the content in chapter 6, "Figuring Out What Happens Next," to explore some of the decisions that will need to be made by survivors as they plan your memorial and do what you can to give them a head start on the process. (In chapter 2, "Making Wishes Known to Loved Ones," you can find more on how to communicate your life story on pages 50–54.)

Your archive is a good place to also address any specific rituals, chants, clothing, or preparation that speaks to your cultural heritage. For instance, in both the Orthodox Jewish and Muslim faiths there are ceremonial washing ceremonies.

In the Hindu faith, an open flame is part of the ceremony of the dead, and for Latter Day Saints, special clothing is required for burial. Many Buddhist cultures insist on whole body burial as the person must remain intact to make the passage into the next life. Some religions request that the body be buried within 24 hours (see "Religious and Cultural Considerations" in the appendix on pages 221–234). And some communities frown on anything other than a three-day affair with open casket, receptions, formal burial in the family plot, and a wake. Perhaps you want to be buried or cremated in a special outfit you cherish. Whatever you wish, a one-page summary should do it. Just let your family know your wishes in advance.

Online Options for End-of-Life Planning

For those digitally minded, there are numerous end-of-life online services to assist including the following:

- *Cake*. Born out of an MIT health care "hackathon" conference,[17] Cake is a free service that catalogs users' end of life plans, documents, and instructions. Want a special playlist at your memorial reception? Do you prefer to be cremated and buried as compost? Is there a favorite beach or river where you would like your ashes to be scattered? Are there specific readings or poems you want to have read at your memorial? Do you want to be pressurized into a diamond after your demise? Their blog includes advance care and end-of-life planning, estate planning, and funeral planning as well as advice on legal and financial matters. Log on and list your choices so your loved ones won't have to guess at https://www.joincake.com.

- *Willing.* Willing is an website that specializes in state-specific estate planning documents. Their complete estate planning package includes a living will, durable power of attorney, last will and testament, revocable living trust, and transfer on death deed (if available in your state). Expect to retire in Big Sky Country? Hook up your spurs in Texas? Live (and die) near the grandkids in Iowa? You can review their package at https://willing.com.

- *Parting.* Parting provides an online directory of nearly 15,000 funeral homes. If a loved one dies unexpectedly in another state and time is of the essence, or if you are looking for the closest and most economical plan for your own funeral, this list is invaluable. The site allows you to search for funeral homes by location, view images, itemize the services, and review costs, and read the reviews at http:// www.parting.com.

- *Lantern.* Calling itself "the single source of guidance for navigating life before and after death,"[18] Lantern offers a free checklist to navigate "what comes next," including preplanning, funeral planning, obituary writing, advice on closing digital accounts, benefits eligibility, and grief and bereavement issues at https:// www.lantern.co.

- *New Narrative Memorials.* This is a virtual funeral and virtual memorial planning company. In the wake of the COVID-19 pandemic, they have teamed up with LifeWeb 360 to provide families a step-by-step planning tool to create a virtual funeral, memorial, or celebration-of-life event including a viewing, a streamed service, or a recording of the funeral and reception at https://www.newnarrative.ca.

Body Disposition Options

For many, body disposition decisions are predicated on cultural heritage and sensibilities. Due to the lack of burial space in many communities and military sites, cremation has become a popular choice. The portability, cost, and storage of cremains is often preferred, especially when the burial is delayed. (During the recent coronavirus pandemic, a Northern California cremation agency noted the wait time to get a death certificate and burial was six weeks.) If survivors plan to scatter cremation remains (cremains), arrangements must be made with the county where the cremains will be scattered and/or make plans with a pilot and aviation group that specializes in flyovers.

In countless cultures and religions, whole-body burial remains the only choice. If this is the case for your family, choose a mortuary or funeral home that performs the specific religious and cultural rituals you desire. Some funeral homes are focused on specific religions. Others provide a diverse variety of services. If you are part of a religious community, church or temple, it's likely you've been to a memorial. Ask friends about their experiences and the burial arrangements.

An emerging preference is to "go green" and choose an ecological solution for the remains of the deceased.

Driven by a preference to consume fewer resources and be more earth friendly, some individuals do not want to continue the former practices of embalming with formaldehyde and other chemicals. They also reject cremation due to the energy consumed and chemicals used. In order to help concerned individuals be more environmentally sensitive, new practices have emerged. Water cremation, freeze-drying, cannibal mushrooms, growing ashes into trees, and ecopod coffins are just a few ecological burial alternatives. Or you can more simply choose to have everything that goes in the ground with your body be as biodegradable as your body itself.

Consider Recompose, a company that specializes in a process that gently converts human remains into soil. The process begins with natural organic reduction that is powered by beneficial microbobes, which occur naturally on the body. As the process continues, the body is laid in a cradle surrounded by wood chips, alfalfa, and straw. Finally, it is placed into a Recompose vessel and covered with more plant material, remaining there for 30 days. Microbes break everything down on the molecular level resulting in a nutrient dense soil. The soil is allowed to cure and then used to enrich conservation land, forests, or gardens (https://recompose.life/our-model).

According to a recent piece in the *New York Times*, a green burial is also a potential way to save money. The median cost of traditional burial is $8755 while the average cost of a green burial runs between $1000 and $4000. If you are interested in these options, now is the time to start looking into what is available in your community and discussing green alternatives with your loved ones.

Outstanding Debts and Regular Ongoing Bills

Many banks allow clients to make automatic bill payments to companies or institutions. Encourage your executor or personal representative to notify the banks and institutions about your death as soon as possible to avoid unnecessary payments. Consider gathering the following information in a one-page summary to include in your archive or binder. Group your information according in the three following categories.

1. List all bills that you are responsible for that are a specific amount and are paid automatically at specific intervals. These might include first and second mortgages, child support or alimony payments, car payments, payments for personal loans from a bank, monthly charitable donations, and bi-monthly or quarterly waste disposal/sewer bills from the city, gym memberships, and streaming services or cable bills.

2. List common bills that are variable in cost and come in monthly (general credit card bills, store credit card bills, phone/internet bill, and utility bills such as electricity, water, etc.).

3. List any personal obligations; debts or liens; tax payments; less regular donations to a church, synagogue, or temple or to charities or an individual; outstanding health care and hospital bills; or unpaid undocumented or unofficial payments/gifts to a family member or any other individual. These usually take the most time to sort out and are the most painful, especially the final hospital bill.

This list of debts will help your survivors update information regarding who needs to be contacted and paid before a summary of estate assets can be formed. Some families assume debt goes away with death. It doesn't. In fact, the worst-case scenario is finding out a dead relative had a huge gambling debt that wasn't paid. Survivors must stay vigilant and, most of all, wait at least six months or more to make any distributions. Survivors are allowed to evaluate the value of the assets of the estate on the date of death or six months later for tax purposes.

Tax Documents

Tax preparers, CPAs (certified public accountants), and enrolled agents all suggest keeping at least seven years of tax returns on hand for potential audits. Also retain records of special purchases, business transactions, and any subsequent changes to be submitted to the IRS due to extraordinary circumstances (an income windfall, unemployment years, disability, etc.). All of these documents belong in your archive. If an estate is audited, it is highly recommended to hire an enrolled agent who is licensed to represent the case in tax court before the IRS. Survivors also need a professional tax expert for the final estate tax filing for the deceased.

Saving Receipts

It's likely that a home sale will occur at some point in the estate process. Hopefully, some wise sage told you early on to keep all the receipts for the permanent repairs, remodels, and upgrades to your home. Keep these receipts in a separate file so when your house is sold, your survivors have a record of what was spent. In these inflationary times, it's good to have these itemized expenses. They can be added to the base price (cost basis) that was paid for the home to reduce capital gains and the associated taxes on those gains. Leaving these records in your archive reduces the headaches of your survivors not knowing where to look for the receipt of the remodel in '87 or the new air conditioning system you put in last year.

You may also have rented out your home or used part of your home as an office. If so, add the tax accounting records to your archive as they may also be used as part of the final accounting for the home.

Whew. You got through the financials. You're way ahead of the average person! Take a break, a nap, eat, maybe even sleep through the night. Then when you are ready, begin addressing estate issues and legal documents in the next section of this chapter.

Cleaning Out the Closet

Have a shield up to protect those you love from "well-meaning" but deceptive relatives and friends who want to tidy-up at the expense of your intended heirs. Consider this cautionary tale.

I once worked with a parishioner whose husband's children wanted their inheritance ASAP and were on her doorstep the day after her spouse died. They were determined to take everything they thought was "theirs." As part of this effort, they were determined to get her out of "their" home so they could sell it. This was cruelty beyond imagination. They rolled up the moving truck to the back door and cleaned out her husband's closets and took the furniture they believed were their "family heirlooms." They informed her she had 14 days to move out and showed her a copy of the mortgage and deed, which only had her husband's name on it. At the memorial she was not invited to the dinner they "hosted."

I sat with my parishioner after this devastation, listened to her deep sadness, and then took an inventory. We tallied up what was left and what she could move forward with. The church found her another apartment, moved her belongings, provided the necessary furniture required to live, and brought in two weeks of groceries plus homemade dishes. She'd had no time to adjust to the loss. Once she was relocated and settled, she was finally able begin the grieving process. The church also provided free counseling sessions and lots and lots of love and friends to make up for the deficit along with a small group of other widows our church-sponsored called "Women with Heart." She could breathe again.

Managing possessions and making inventories of things eliminates so much of the heartache that occurs after a death, especially in blended families. Take the time now to sort out the legal and emotional landmines before others assume something is theirs.

Legal and Estate Information

As noted, this list of essential documents and information is divided into financial information and legal and estate matters. Now I address the legal matters.

The Will

Your will is the basic document that determines how your property will be distributed upon your death to beneficiaries/heirs. A will also specifies who the guardian of any minor children will be. Note that not all of your assets are distributed through a will; some, such as IRA accounts and insurance, are distributed according to beneficiary designations kept with the issuing institution or account custodian. As mentioned on pages 92–95, you must contact these other organizations to ensure all assets are distributed according to your wishes.

To establish the validity of your will, a court proceeding called probate is normally required along with a court appearance with an appointed executor and attorneys in fact. (An attorney in fact is a person who is authorized to act on behalf of another person, usually to perform business or other official transactions; these are the people to whom you assigned power of attorney.) Probate can be very expensive as there is a schedule of fees that must be paid based on the estate assets.

In some states, a holographic, handwritten will witnessed by two people and your original signature will suffice. A so-called holographic will is a handwritten and testator-signed document and is an alternative to a will produced by a lawyer. (A testator is a person who has made a will or given a legacy.) Some states do not recognize holographic wills. States that do permit holographic wills require the document meet specific requirements to be valid. With anything of a legal nature, check with your attorney or legal aid office to make sure that whatever document you sign is legal and binding and reflects your wishes. A second opinion can be invaluable.

Trust Documents

A living trust is a legal document created during your lifetime. In this document, a designated person, called the trustee whom you select and name, is given responsibility for managing assets for the benefit of the trust's eventual beneficiary. A living trust can hold your assets while you are alive. The person you appoint as trustee holds the title to the trust property and the beneficiary is the person who receives the benefits of the trust. When you die or become mentally incapacitated, the named successor trustee steps in and manages the assets.

There are two major types of trusts, revocable and irrevocable. Revocable trusts are created during the lifetime of the trust maker and can be altered, changed, modified, or even revoked in their entirety by the trust creator (you). A lot of people find these trusts extremely helpful because if an asset is in the trust, the asset will generally not be subject to probate costs or court process delays. However, even if assets are transferred into a revocable trust, the assets in the trust are subject to the trust maker's creditors, as well as income and estate taxes.

An irrevocable trust is one where the terms of the trust cannot be altered, changed, modified, or revoked after its creation, except with permission of the beneficiary(ies). While rules can vary, once assets are transferred to an irrevocable trust, the trust maker generally can no longer access the property or money for personal use. The benefit is that the assets in an irrevocable trust are effectively removed from the trust maker's estate and are no longer part of their estate for tax purposes. To set up and maintain trusts, engage the services of a competent attorney.

The various kinds of trusts are listed here:

- *Asset protection trust* protects a person's assets from claims of future creditors.

- *A charitable trust* benefits a particular charity.

- *A constructive or implied trust* is established by a court.

- *A special needs trust* is for a person who receives government benefits, but it is set up so as not to disqualify the beneficiary from those benefits.

- *A spendthrift trust* is for the heir who has trouble managing money.

- *A tax bypass trust* limits the amount of tax that would be payable upon the death of a second spouse.

- *A totem trust* is payable upon the death of the grantor.

Again, because of the sensitive and legal nature of these trusts, make sure to find a competent attorney who understands your specific needs to help you establish any trusts.

Power of Attorney (POA) for Finances

As discussed in chapter 3, "Talking about Health and Illness," on pages 77–80, a power of attorney (POA) is written authorization to represent or act on someone else's behalf in business and/or legal matters. A power of attorney for finances deals with your financial and legal matters. This document declares who will handle your finances, accounting, general welfare, and maintenance and notes specific provisions for carrying out your wishes. The personal representative (also called an attorney in fact) may be given the authorization to handle your bank account, pay bills, and work with professionals to manage your affairs. Please note, power of attorney documents do not cover the duties of a personal fiduciary, a person who acts in the best interest of the individual managing assets for a fee on behalf of another or a conservator, who is appointed to handle critical financial decisions after a person is declared incompetent or incapacitated. Also note that a health care proxy has the authority to make medical decisions, whereas a power of attorney has the authority to make financial decisions.

Durable Power of Attorney (POA) for Health Care, Advance Directive for Health Care, HIPAA Authorization, and POLST

We've already covered these in chapter 3, "Talking about Health and Illness," on pages 77–82, so this is just another reminder to make sure that you have these forms completed and that these important documents make the inventory and are included in your archive or binder. Your POLST should be on your refrigerator or in a prominent place.

Other Important Information

In addition to financial and legal information, there are other details your family needs to know about after your death.

Military Service Information

If you are a veteran, first of all, thank you for your service. We can never thank our veterans enough for the sacrifices they have made for our country. And thankfully, your experience comes with some benefits. In your archive, you will need to have the DD214 document accessible which is given to a veteran upon discharge. Along with that document, you will need a copy of your birth certificate, Social Security number, military serial number, military branch affiliation (navy, army, etc.), dates of service, date of birth, and full legal name. Without this information, your heirs will be at the mercy of the Department of Veterans Affairs, which can delay your memorial plans and burial. Your benefits include a military burial at a national cemetery site, a plot or niche in a memorial wall or crypt, and the services of the staff to maintain your place of burial. Because many military sites are filled or have long waiting lists, check in advance to see what site might be available and inform your heirs. The Veteran's Administration will set a day for the memorial (usually a 30-minute service) and most offer a volunteer corps to play taps, present the flag to a family member, and provide a map to locate the burial site. You may also qualify for reimbursement or financial allotment for funeral services. If you can't find your records, www .archives.gov/veterans/military-service-records/ can assist you. In the event you are unable to have a military service, you may wish to receive a burial flag, which you can request through the Veteran's Administration at https://www.va.gov/burials-memorials /memorial-items/burial-flags/.

Personal Gifts

You may have special collections, artwork, and memorabilia that don't fit into any traditional asset category. You may also have a specific thing you want to pass on to one child and not to another. For instance, I had a beautiful engagement/wedding ring from my first marriage. The only person that should have it is my son from that marriage. Therefore, I have listed the ring in my personal wishes and gifts list. Similarly, my husband has a special Civil War artifact that he specified that his son from his first marriage should get. Make a list of things that fit this category and sign and date the list. This will put your mind at rest and prevent ugly arguments.

Pets

You will want your animal companions taken care of when you are no longer there to do so. Contact the people in your circle of support who might be able to care for your pets and ask if they would be willing to do so. If they say yes, be sure to provide information such as the name of your veterinarian and hospital, where you buy pet food, feeding and exercise schedule, and any other pertinent information. For the most devoted of pet owners, there are trusts you can establish. There are books that can tell you how to do so that have other ideas to help protect your pet after your death (one is *Pet Protection Legal Care Plan: Financial and Legal Planning to Protect Our Companion Pets* by Mary G. Anderson). If you are unable to gain permission from someone to care for your animal, you may wish to list adoption agencies or animal shelters nearby.

Original Documents

So far, we've listed items that could fit into a binder or be scanned to include in a digital archive for a hard drive or the cloud. But there are also some original signed documents that must be set aside for legal purposes. You may wish to rent a safety deposit box at a bank to store these items. But as anyone knows who has have ever tried to remove the contents of a safety deposit box after the death of the renter, it can be difficult to do so due to banking and trustee rules. One option is to purchase a a fireproof box for your home that can be moved in the event of an emergency. And be sure to give someone you trust a separate key so they have access. Even if a box like this remains behind in a fire or flood, the contents will survive.

The following list itemizes what needs to be placed in a safety deposit or fireproof box or safe:

- Adoption papers

- Automobile title/bill of sale

- Birth certificate

- Church records (baptism, confirmation)

- Citizenship papers

- Contracts (originals), notes, or debts

- Copyrights and patents

- Custody papers to prove legal guardianship of children

- Death certificates/death records/burial plot deeds

- Divorce records

- Government savings bonds

- Investment documents (certificates, contracts)

- Keys

- Life insurance policies/companies/account numbers/ agents names and numbers

- Marriage records

- Military service records

- Passport

- Real estate papers, abstract, deeds, and mortgages

- Retirement records

- Social Security card/ Medicare numbers

- Will and trust documents (original and signed)

User Names, User IDs, Passwords, PINs, Codes, Etc.

There are countless families I have counseled who are still searching for passwords or encryption numbers for computers, online accounts, and cell phones six months to a year after a person dies. To prevent this, make a simple list noting account numbers, with accompanying user names, user IDs, PINs, passcodes, and passwords. You might also want to list other sensitive and private information in this document that survivors will need to put your affairs to rest including information about any military service, you mother's maiden name, your social security number, your birthplace and birthdate, and your current address. **Most importantly, put this list in a place other than the binder or archive where you list all your assets and account numbers. Your appointed representative or executor is the only person who needs to know where your list of passwords is located.**

Note that Facebook and other social media applications allow you to designate a person to act as your proxy when you die. Go online and sign up your post-death designated driver. To assist in retrieving your online passwords, Google has a special section in settings called "passwords" that may save time.

Getting Your House in Order: Next Steps

Gathering all this together to create your personal archive may seem like a lot of work, but it can be done. Any problem is easier to solve if you attack it step by step.

First Step: What Do You Have?

The documents I discuss in this chapter may seem like an endless list, but I'm guessing you have a lot of these papers, maybe just not in one place or not in the order I list them. Do yourself a favor and get started on figuring out what you have and what you still need. Set aside some time you know you won't be disturbed. Pour a glass of your favorite beverage, put on some great music, consider the checklist we've provided in this chapter on pages 89–90 and in the appendix on page 207, and assume that's your table of contents for the book you are creating. Gather all the documents you have readily available on your desk, the floor, or the bed and begin to organize them in the order of the checklist. Check off what you have (patting yourself on the back) and make a list of what is missing. Put everything in a pile and add sheets of colored paper tabs for each of the various categories, or just stack them up and sort on your own.

Second Step: What's Missing?

Take a breath. Once you have checked the boxes for the items you do have, you can begin to prioritize what you need to complete your checklist and who you need to contact to fill in the gaps. Keep in mind that you probably don't need every document on the checklist. Some folks, for example, are fine with just a will and have no plans for a trust. Others forego life insurance based on their age and family's needs. The whole exercise of putting your house in order is a big task and it's going to take time. If you are feeling that your tank is low on energy right now, your heirs may have to figure some of this out on their own, but the whole process will be much further along if you are able to begin the effort to gather as much information as possible in one place.

Third Step: Finding the Professionals Who Can Help You Fill in the Gaps

For taxes, audits, and final tax returns, find an enrolled agent or CPA who is skilled in accounting and the fine art of defending people before the IRS. A generic tax preparer is generally okay, but not recommended for complicated estate matters.

For legal work (wills, trusts, powers of attorney, and specialized trusts) find a lawyer who comes with personal recommendations, is fully licensed by the state bar, and specializes in estate planning. Yes, you can do some of the work yourself, but if you are concerned about probate court or have a contentious family member who may argue over distributions, a lawyer is your friend. Be sure to ask how the lawyers you interview bill their time (court time, phone calls, meetings, and research) and get that information in writing. It's likely you will be asked to pay money upfront (called a retainer). Gather any documents they ask to see in advance of meeting with them to save time and, hopefully, additional fees.

For financial matters, opt for a fee-only planner who is willing to organize and develop a portfolio that is easy to understand that the planner will update per your wishes. (Quarterly updates are generally the norm with a face-to-face meeting once a year.) A person who has obtained a Certified Financial Planner (CFP) or Personal Financial Planner (PFP) designation and who is not interested in commissions, but works with a fee or percentage structure, is generally someone who is looking out for your best interest. Be bold. Ask any financial planners you interview how they make their money and ask them if they help with matters beyond simple portfolio management and investments. A good financial planner can be a valuable ally, educating and encouraging you to make decisions that will help you now and your heirs in the future.

In insurance, there are three worlds, and they are pretty much all commission-based. There are brokers who handle property and liability insurance (cars, homes, and accidents), life insurance brokers, and brokers for health insurance (hospital, disability, clinics, doctors, prescriptions, etc.). For many people, a health insurance broker, working on behalf of your employer, creates their family coverage. Others have joined the Medicare health care insurance universe and have premium deductions taken out of their bank accounts monthly. However, most people are generally on their own with property and liability and life insurance. Ask your friends for brokers they would recommend. Seek positive personal testimonies and long-term relationships, and compare rates and prices.

As a general rule, before embarking on any professional relationship, it is a good idea is to interview at least three people and find out who is the best fit for you. Although your best friend Jerry may have found someone to be efficient and personable, that same broker or planner may prove to be a nightmare for you. Take the time and choose wisely. It's likely the people you choose to help you with these matters will be the bridge between your final inventories and your family's future well-being.

Congratulations! You've made it to the end of this chapter! Although this process can be exhausting, if you have collected as much of this information in one place as you possibly can, you have just saved your executor and loved ones months of work.

CHAPTER
5

Saying Goodbye and the Dying Process

Our ultimate goal, after all, is not a good death, but a good life to the very end.

—Atul Gawande

Most people say that we are all in the process of dying. I say that until we are dead, we are in the process of living. Dying is our final act of living.

—Barbara Karnes

You matter because you are you, and you matter to the last moment of your life. We will do all we can, not only to help you die peacefully but also live until you die.

—Dame Cicely Saunders
(founder of the modern
hospice movement)

Angela

As per protocol, nurses on the unit called the chaplain to visit a patient who had transitioned to the last stages of life, or comfort care. Normally these moments are spent satisfying the wishes of the family and making sure prayers and rituals are performed. The chaplains often stay a few moments to comfort the family in their pre-loss and answer any questions about post-death matters. However, this visit was different. Visiting with the patient's nurse outside her room, I learned that at 93, this patient, Angela, had pretty much done it all. An educator, Shakespearean actress, and musical comedy star in her community theatre, she had a successful marriage, had three children and multiple grandchildren, and was a lot of fun.

Now, however, the medical heroics were over. Angela was barely able to hold her head up a bit, sip small slurps of water from the spongy lollipop and open her eyes when the family arrived. As I sat through the difficult family meeting listening to the doctors saying that they'd done everything possible and that there were no more options, my mind began to wander.

I was recalling every musical I had ever seen performed in my childhood and adult years. Once the medical team left the room, I asked the family if it would be okay if we had a songfest to send Angela out. Permission granted. For the next hour, I (along with the daughters when they remembered the lyrics) sang tunes from *Damn Yankees, The Sound of Music, The Phantom of the Opera, South Pacific, West Side Story, Annie Get Your Gun* as well old classic hymns such as "Amazing Grace," "Great Is Thy Faithfulness," and "How Great Thou Art." Nurses stopped their routines and moved closer to Angela's door. The cleaning attendant lifted her mop and looked up. Doctors halted their rounds and came to the end of the hall. For a few moments, the hospital was Broadway. No one wanted to leave. Exhausted, I realized we'd already spent an hour together. After a brief prayer, I excused myself so the family could be alone with the patient. About a day and a half later Angela died. I have no idea how much of the concert Angela listened to, but I know that hearing is the last thing to go.

Delun

Delun's mother was clutching her prayer beads. His father was pacing the floor, chanting softly in the darkened room. Their 17-year-old son was lying in bed still breathing without the ventilator but very still. Delun's mother requested a Buddhist priest to manage the last rites of prayers, the golden blanket, chanting, and anointing for his journey to the next world. Pictures, bookmarks with tassels, and small statues of Buddha adorned his room, which was slowly taking the form of a shrine. I had given Delun's parents a few recorded chants to soothe their sorrowful hearts as they watched their son slip into the coma from which he would not awake. And when Delun died, I asked the nurses to turn off all the machines, lower the bed, and to disengage the room's mechanics and hydraulics to leave the family in silence. They sat vigil and relatives were welcome to come and support the transition. Although their faith designated that they needed three days, Delun's family were allowed to be in his hospital room only eight hours following his death. They asked and were granted permission to remove his body to their home to finish the three-day rite.

Your Chapter 5 Checklist:

1. Learn about new tools for communicating with friends and family during extended illness.

2. Consider your visiting options and best practices when a loved one is ill or nearing death.

3. Learn the importance of saying goodbye and how to say goodbye.

4. Explore what happens in the last days and hours of death.

Note that the first four chapters in the book are addressed to the person who may be facing a diagnosis that is terminal. In contrast, this chapter is more geared to the needs of the survivors. But for the person who is dying, knowing what their survivors may be facing can be helpful, and knowing what the wishes of a loved one are can make the last days to months a little easier for everyone who is touched by the death. When people know and express the kinds of care they desire (or don't desire), their general and specific religious preferences and the rituals they want performed, the people they want near them, and the things that bring them joy, this time period can both honor the life that is ending and facilitate the tough work of saying goodbye.

I don't believe anyone looks forward to planning out the last days of a life. But I do believe everyone wants to do what they can to make the last days as pleasant and manageable as possible. Think of this chapter as a guideline, offering advice on how to plan, structure, organize, and delegate the tasks of living at the end of life.

CaringBridge: Communicating about Events, Progress, and Concerns

Caring for someone who is ill can be overwhelming. And trying to keep relatives and friends up to date on all the medical news is even harder. CaringBridge is an online global nonprofit social network that helps alleviate some of that stress. It allows you to build a personal website or mobile app with all the tools you need to keep family and friends updated about a patient's status. A caregiver or patient can report on treatments or the progress of an illness whether care is given at home or in the hospital. Friends and family who sign up to be informed can respond, encourage, and write letters or tributes to the patient or family. This eliminates the endless calls or e-mails people used to have to make to "catch up" on a patient's progress. Friends and family can even print daily correspondence and information so people who are less computer savvy can also stay informed. You can set boundaries, ask for and organize help with running errands, preparing food, or doing home and garden chores. Patients and caregivers can respond to questions and offers of help as their time allows, not whenever a phone rings or an e-mail pings them. Everyone is on the same page with a fraction of the effort.

Positive Visitation

Many people have questions about how to behave in the face of illness or death. Thankfully, it is not a situation that many people find themselves in often, so it can be hard to know what to do. In this section, I share some ideas about visiting in person and visiting virtually that can make things go more smoothly for the patient, the caregivers, and the visitors.

Visiting in Person

If a patient is confined to a hospital bed for the duration, the following content introduces a few helpful ideas for people who are able to visit:

- Visitors should check in with the nurse to ask about ways they can be helpful to the patient or caregivers. Sometimes nurses can mention things they have enjoyed in the past. You may find that music or watching a brief video together is acceptable or just listening to a special concert on the radio or TV would be a nice break for the patient.

- Less is often more when it comes to visits. It is not helpful to insist on spending the better part of an hour wearing out a patient who is under sedation and struggling to communicate. Be brief and remain positive and caring. If there are no restrictions regarding social distancing or touching, hold their hand, brush their forehead, or massage their arm, whatever seems appropriate and loving. Sit at eye level and speak loudly enough that they can easily hear you. Watch for signs of fatigue so you can excuse yourself gracefully before the patient is overtired.

- If appropriate, acknowledge religious preferences, perhaps by saying a prayer, reading a devotional or special poem, or singing a favorite song, hymn, or chant to lift the spirits of the patient or the family. Whatever you decide to do while you are there, remember your presence is your gift to them. Sometimes the best visit is spent in silence and the best gift is your smile. Be present in the moment and make the most of your time. ("Religious and Cultural Considerations" on pages 221–234 may help you identify appropriate activities.)

- Scan the room and find ways to affirm the environment. Allow the environment to begin the conversation. Once I visited a room with numerous pieces of artwork piled on the patient's tray table. I asked permission to hang them over the windows of her room to create an art gallery. The patient was thrilled, and the staff admired the resident artist.

- Consider asking about inviting a special visitor if appropriate. Special visitors in a hospital might include a musician who is skilled in music therapy. These folks can match the music to the setting, patient, or requests. Many hospitals employ an art therapist for sketching, watercolor painting, or colored drawings. Or check in with guest services to see if a dog visitor is available. Something almost spiritual occurs when a sweet canine enters the room and a patient can spend time stroking their coat or speaking to them.

- Be sure to acknowledge the family or caregiver who may get little credit or support for their long and sometimes thankless vigil. Introduce yourself to anyone else who is present in the room and let others know how you know the patient and how they have influenced your life. Give caregivers affirmation for the time they've spent with their loved one. As appropriate, offer to sit with the patient while the caregiver(s) takes a break for coffee or a meal. You can also offer to bring a meal for the family so they can take a break away from the patient's room and save the on-going costs of meals away from home.

- Take the time to peruse the room before you leave to see if there is something that may be appreciated or needed.

It might be photos, books, items from their home, cards, letters, or anything personal that will bring comfort. Do they seem to enjoy having flowers, cards, or personal touches around? Are their blankets the standard hospital issue; could you provide an upgrade? What about devices to play music, videos, or audible books? Make a mental inventory and consider what you might be able bring to the room (with family and nursing staff's permission, of course) to make it more personal. That said, do keep in mind there are countless restrictions about personal objects and gifts in many facilities. For instance, flowers may be forbidden due to allergens and critical care units have very little space for personal items that might get in the way during an emergency procedure. Check first, and then make a subsequent visit and bring the surprise.

Kathy and Herb

I recall the day I visited my friends Kathy and Herb at home:

Determined to celebrate 33 years of marriage, Kathy invited me to their condo. Her husband, Herb, was dressed in a diaper, feet draped over a pillow because of two recently discovered bed sores. His head rested on a nest of pillows; there were no blankets covering him. His brow was feverish and he was alternating between small body tremors that arose from time to time and peace. Kathy was in her caregiver garb—a comfortable tee and jeans. Her hair slightly was disheveled, but in place. The living room was scattered with packages of adult diapers, miscellaneous medicines, and cracker crumbs. A parrot named Sydney, who was happy to interrupt, rounded out the tableau. Two lovely bouquets were present: one in the window near the light was from a brother-in-law and one on the table was from a friend. The flower vases were nestled in with the bills and hospice caregivers' business cards.

We began our time together seated in front of Herb, catching up on news, sharing a bit about a wedding I'd just observed and about ceremonies in general. I noticed their wedding pictures were missing from the celebration and commented on this. Kathy quickly retrieved two small frames from the mantle and put them on the table. Inspired, she held one up to Herb and he tried to open one eye. Kathy continued to describe their wedding day at the church and laughed about the hats and the lace so popular at that time, but Herb didn't move. He was silent and held his head turned slightly away from the light. We had hoped he would be able to hear the memories of how handsome he looked in his tux and what a beautiful bride Kathy was. Working off the wedding theme, I decided to read from Revelation 21 and 22, about the bride and the church, and began to paint a picture of heaven. Herb's posture appeared to change; I believed that he heard what I was reading.

At that moment, it occurred to me it might be nice to renew their wedding vows. I mentioned the idea to Herb, and for the first time in three days, Herb's fragile hand raised to meet Kathy's. He was ready to hold her hand as he repeated the vows. I asked Kathy to repeat her vows first, and then Herb's lips moved and he recited all of his vows. Kathy began to cry. Fighting back my own tears, I asked Kathy if I could anoint Herb's head with oil in the tradition of James, and she agreed it would be comforting to pray. I prayed for strength, peace, and solace, for Kathy's health and spirits, for friends to come and visit, and for this day to be special and memorable. Then I remembered a beautiful rendition of the song "Be Still My Soul" and found the recording on my phone. It is a heartfelt song sung by a David Archeluta trying to understand God's will; playing it brought a certain solace, a peace to the room. Both Kathy and I closed our eyes to listen to the last verse which includes these lines:

> *Be still my soul, when change and tears are past*
>
> *All safe and blessed we shall meet at last.*

Kathy bent over the bed and started to cry much bigger tears, finally letting go, exhibiting the deeply embedded sorrow she was feeling on her anniversary as she watched her husband slowly slip away. I encouraged her to let go and allow me to comfort her. She was not alone, and we were celebrating the 33 years of uncomplicated loving devotion. Honest, brittle moments like this remind me of the true commitment we make when we vow, "'til death do us part."

When Visitors Can't Be Present in Person: Long Distance or Isolation Visits

Sometimes people can't drive or fly to be with important people during hard times or the end of life. The recent global pandemic has forced many of us to be creative. If visitors and well-wishers are unable to visit a hospital, facility, or home in person, the following suggestions may be useful.

- Find out what would be appreciated by the patient and do some research to make sure someone can deliver it. A special blanket or socks adorned with pictures of their favorite animal might be a start. Or send a fun hat to wear after chemotherapy sessions.

- If there are certain foods the patient is still allowed to eat, make a favorite recipe and send the treat along with a personal note.

- Hold a video family meal. Set up a Zoom meeting or video chat at a time appropriate for the patient's mealtime. Encourage corny jokes and family humor.

- Create a playlist of the patient's favorite performer or genre of music. You can do this alone or encourage other family members to come up with their favorites and write a dedication to the patient. Although receiving a playlist is great fun for the recipient, it's also a lift for family and friends to collaborate and collect.

- Take advantage of video call options. Skype, Facetime, or Zoom are wonderful alternatives to voice-only communication. Many hospitals provide patients with an iPad and internet access. And even members of the older generations are moving to smartphone communication. Explore what's possible. Many families set a specific time to meet weekly (for example, 5:30 p.m. Sunday night). If your friend group or family is musically inclined, singing and playing music together in real time is another endorphin boost. Just make sure everyone has their own set of earbuds or headsets to avoid unnecessary noise or interference for others in the area. If you have a little more time, and someone in your family can handle the technical expertise of editing, record a song as a family.

- Make a recording of people praising the patient's character and best qualities. Have everyone talk about one aspect of a person's life that has touched them. Is the patient kind, creative, generous, and talented? Ask the people in the patient's life to tell a story to illustrate a quality and compile the tapes as a video. To share these messages, consider using a video communication app such as Marco Polo, which is a video recorder that captures and stores brief face-to-face calls. When the recipient has time to watch, they can call up your recording.

All the things I note here are merely suggestions. You may have more creative ways to celebrate the life of your family member, friend, or colleague. Think about what the patient has meant to you, check in with their family, and be creative to find a way to reach out that works.

Saying Goodbye and Witnessing Death

I often advise people to strive to arrange to see a person as soon as they hear that death is imminent. Do not delay. Even if you believe a person's spirit is present after they expire, it's still emotionally difficult to speak to a dead person. A goodbye visit is your chance to affirm the good things in their life and offer your blessing over a person. This is your opportunity to say the things you'd may have hoped to say before this point but never got the chance. This is the time to witness and offer words of honor and tribute. If the person is a believer, these are moments to talk about heaven or the afterlife and the spiritual home to come. And this is the moment you can offer the final hug or hand squeeze and look a person in the eyes to let them know they are loved.

Saying goodbye is important. Most medical personnel would agree that the last sense to fail is hearing. Allow your words to be filled with love. Say what is in your heart and you can be at peace knowing that you had the chance to share your feelings with the dying person while they were still alive. Ira

Byock, in his book *The Four Things That Matter Most*, notes that people need to communicate four things to each other: "Please forgive me," "I forgive you," "thank you," and "I love you."[19] These four sentiments are a good beginning, but also think about the specific and personal things that you what you want to declare to this person. What would you like to be the last affirming words they hear from you? This should not be a scripted speech, just things from your heart, sweet recollections, and funny anecdotes touching idioms or sayings, songs, or memories of a shared history. If you get a chance to say goodbye in person, even if you don't make it to the memorial, your heart will be at rest. You were part of their send-off.

The Last Days: Communication and Solace

I often say to families, "The body speaks long before we do." Simply put, when a person is actively in the process of dying, the body will decide when it is ready to go. Even if all the observers and the patient themselves does not know exactly what will happen next, the body may. In general, people who are dying need help with four areas: achieving physical comfort; meeting mental and emotional needs; addressing spiritual issues; and taking care of practical tasks.[20]

Some patients may feel depressed or anxious and need reassuring conversations about their feelings. Dying people also may have fears and concerns about being alone, isolated, and have no one to talk to due to lack of family or support. They may also fear for those they are leaving behind and may need assurance that those they are leaving will be okay. They may feel a sudden need to make confessions or heal past relationships or have time with a spiritual leader. Honor their requests as you can and find professionals who can help. Honor these, their final wishes. Ask them, "What would help you now?"

Remember their physical and emotional needs as well. Warm your fingers and hold a hand or gently rub a back. Use gentle touch to affirm presence and caring. Set a mood with soft song sung in a low volume or softly play an instrumental recording of a song the patient knows and loves. These gestures of love often help with relaxation and improve mood; they can even lessen the pain. Tell some stories, read to them, honor their worth, and let them how they have influenced you and mentored and loved you.

Some people who are dying are resilient and fight the process. They thrust their fists into the air and defy nature, saying it won't happen. I have encountered patients who will find any means to sustain for a few days or weeks more. Other folks simply accept their situation and begin to decline, or purposely refuse to respond, eat, or hydrate. There is no set way to predict or control this time (unless someone has chosen physician aid in the dying process or a doctor and the family have decided to take a person off life support).

When a person is actively in the process of dying, the trajectory is typically a few days to a week, and doctors order comfort care to be provided. When the patient has stopped eating and drinking with any regularity, a plan is put in place to keep them comfortable, dry, and reasonably hydrated. Forcing food or liquids at this point can be detrimental as it builds up unnecessary fluids in the body and can create further discomfort. The objective of comfort care is to provide a comfortable, pain-free time with some space for communicating with family and friends if possible. The doctors are no longer trying to find ways to keep the body functioning and, more often than not, a person's vital organs are shutting down. In most cases, patients are able to communicate if the airway is not obstructed, but they may also use a writing tablet if speech is difficult. This is the time you put the call out to those who want to come and say their final words. Hospice or hospital personnel actively involved in the patient's care will honor your time with your loved one.

Saying Difficult Things

The emotional temperature of a family is hard to predict at this time. Some estranged relatives will show up unexpectedly to pay respects and be in mental chaos, spouting resentment and anger about an unresolved issue. Others may pour themselves over a bed lamenting they never had the chance to say the things they wanted to say. Or the patient may want to set the record straight and confess to an unknown past or take the time to reconcile with a child or former relationship. A family member can act as a point person and soften the blow or discuss things in advance when they see a person about to enter a room. A chaplain may also be a neutral third party if the communication is slipping into judgment or inappropriate magical thinking.

The Chaplain's Role: Spiritual Comfort

If a death is imminent in your family, take time to get to know the chaplain (or other religious figure) in your medical facility and utilize their services. As a person who has been in the chaplain's position for many years, I know that people are still unsure as to what a chaplain does, whether in a hospice/palliative care/nursing home setting or in a hospital. Chaplains are the bridge to meaning and purpose, relationships that need healing. We may serve as a connector for the embedded faith of childhood and a counselor to aid in ending disagreements. Here's a short list of what chaplains can provide at end of life:

- Discuss a person's faith background and preferences, meaning and purpose, goals, joys, and concerns about forgiveness and regrets.

- Assist with reaching out to a faith-specific practitioner (for example, an imam, Buddhist priest, guru, rabbi, pastor, or a person who provides spiritual guidance in a specific language).

- Provide a priest for anointing of the sick or reconciliation for a Catholic patient.

- Provide presence and solace to grieving family and friends.

- Perform rituals including prayers, readings, singing, or Eucharist or communion as appropriate.

- Encourage survivors to gather and record thoughts of those present and share them in the form of tribute or remembrances of the person who is dying.

- Allow people to process their feelings without feeling inhibited.

- Sit with the primary caregiver and offer one-on-one solace and empathy.

- In some hospitals, arrange for a volunteer from No One Dies Alone/No One Alone (NODA/NOA), programs that provide the reassuring presence of a volunteer companion to dying patients who would otherwise be alone, to sit with a dying patient.

- Contact the Threshold Choir (a national musical organization that provides volunteer singers to sing for people on the thresholds of living and dying) for musical comfort and peaceful songs.

- Communicate the patient's religious burial wishes to the medical staff so they know what rituals, silence, prayers, or remembrances are required for the patient or family at the time of death (see chapter 3, "Talking about Health and Illness," page 77–82).

The Last Sprint

Often, just when you think a person is actively dying, the dying person may experience an unexpected jolt of life. A person in their final days may suddenly gain an inordinate amount of energy and want to take one more lap around the track. Your loved one may abruptly transition from a listless existence to a more energetic one. They may suddenly rise up and want a party or a gathering. They may ask you to arrange a special event to say goodbye with as many dear ones present as possible. If it's possible, try to make it happen. But be aware that this may not be the moment for a profound exchange of last words like in the movies. Most people simply sense the need for one last moment to celebrate life with those they love.

A Last Hurrah

I remember a parishioner who had been languishing in bed for weeks. One day, she decided she was done. She wanted her whole family bedside. According to her wishes, her family and I staged the celebration, told stories, snuck in some champagne, and even served a few patient-selected snacks forbidden by the hospice staff. When we were done laughing and singing around 9 p.m., the patient sent everyone home. Her final wish had been granted. Just after noon the next day, she died. It was exactly the way she wanted it. Then her husband, also infirmed and lying just ten feet from her death bed, took his turn. He stopped eating and drinking and died 16 days later.

Some people have an uncanny sense of timing or simply will themselves to finish on their own terms. They know what is going on internally and physically. They have the power and spiritual awareness to know when it is their time. What a gift to stage your own wake.

The Finish Line

When a body slips into a coma or semicomatose state and communication is no longer an option, a waiting period or vigil often takes place. Some families choose to have a family member present around the clock in the room with the dying person. Others may decide to take a break and wait to receive a call at the time of death. At some facilities, volunteers from No One Dies Alone/No One Alone may be the person in the room when a patient dies. Most people would choose not to die alone. I've been in hospital rooms and hospice homes when the whole family arrives and sings hymns, reads scripture, and prays. I've also been in darkened rooms filled with soft music and the low chanting of Buddhist prayers.

If you attend a death, you may notice many things about the dying person in these last few hours: a change in skin color; labored breathing that has a "rattle" or congested sound; some irritation and movement in the bed; short breaths and agitated head or leg movement; a change in the body temperature of extremities such as the head, hands, and feet; and even a few words or sounds. The dying person's body is making its last communications with this earth and taking its final breaths. What can the living who are present do at this time? Be with your dying loved ones. Come alongside them. Talk with them, touch their hands, wipe their forehead, and, as the nurse allows, swab their mouth for moisture or offer ice chips, rearrange blankets, play soothing music, or guard the silence.

Most importantly, be there. Be a presence. Let them know they are not alone. When a person dies, it is a sacred moment.

Figuring Out
What Happens Next

Transitions are almost always signs of growth, but they can bring feelings of loss. To get somewhere new, we may have to leave somewhere else behind.

—Fred Rogers

The end of life even in the midst of a crisis should be a sacred time.

—Dr. Betty Ferrell, Director of Nursing Research and Education, City of Hope Comprehensive Cancer Center

Leroy

The call came in about 10:00 p.m. from my brother-in-law Frank. It was, as I predicted, about my dad, Leroy. He'd been frail and failing for some time, and Frank's voice was adamant. I could hear my mother and sister crying in the background. It was clear I needed to get on the next flight out, but I couldn't find a flight till morning. All I could do that night was wait and try to sleep for a few fretful hours. Somehow, lying there that night, I knew I would be too late. I would not see my dad alive again.

The second call came in about an hour later to let me know my father was dead. My husband called our pastor, who wanted to speak to me, but I couldn't hold the phone. Boarding the plane the next morning, I felt totally devastated. When I arrived, Dad's body was already in the morgue. My mother was almost completely silent; my sister was in tears. All my mother could say is that she wanted me to go and see him. I couldn't. I wanted to remember him the way he was. I wanted to remember my hero, not some pale, naked body on a slab. I could feel her frustration with me and her anger rising, but I stood my ground. This was my dad, and I needed to hold on to the good.

I would later lead the charge for getting the service ready. As a pastor, I'd already officiated at dozens of memorials and knew the drill. I also knew the officiating pastor who was in charge at my parents' church. But now, there were seemingly hundreds of details that had to be addressed to prepare a body for the burial. Looking back, I wish I had known more and that my parents had prepared a little better. As it was, we were adrift in a sea of mortuaries, morticians, crematoriums, polite coercion, endless details, death certificates, and sadness. Nothing had been set in place. I was at square one.

Ellen

When my sister-in-law Ellen was in her last hours, we were all in the hospital room, aware that her death was imminent and trying to remain vigilant. The room was silent. Ellen's son, Jeremy, went for a walk with his youth pastor, Matt, and came up with a playlist. It featured a sweet praise song with a few verses and it was topped it off with Bon Jovi's "Living on a Prayer." It was a transformational moment. From a deep sadness of pre-loss, we started singing along with the staff at the top of our lungs with gusto. Irreverent? Hardly. This was Ellen's young son's way of saying the goodbye. It was his personal way of celebrating her life. I truly believe she was in that moment. Less than a half-hour later, Ellen died. Jeremy stroked her hair and hands, and family members cried softly and held each other. My brother, Ellen's husband, sat in disbelief and wept. No one really had the words or any agenda anymore. What was clear was that we celebrated her life to the end.

Your Chapter 6 Checklist:

1. Learn more what happens to a body after death—including information about medical and legal procedures and religious concerns and preparations.

2. Review the responsibilites of a personal representative/agent.

3. Understand common options for interment and inurnment and some of the costs involved.

4. Explore personal ways to celebrate the life of a loved one with family and friends.

When a person dies, it is a sacred moment. In the medical community, they often practice what they call "the pause," which is a moment of silence. The staff that is present pauses to recognize the dignity of a life lived. Some pray silently, others bow their heads, some hug a person next to them, or some simply remain silent. This ritual recognizes that every person matters. At the moment of death, the people who are present realize their own mortality.

This chapter covers what happens after the pause. Note that this chapter, like the proceeding chapter (chapter 5, "Saying Goodbye and the Dying Process"), is addressed primarily to survivors instead of the person who is dying.

There are few moments more disconcerting than those that follow death. Death may occur in a variety of circumstances. It may follow a prolonged time of suffering or a brief but heroic attempt to save a life after an accident. It may be a fitting end to a life well lived or be the result of a homicide. Some families are in agony and others may be relieved. What is common to all these scenarios is the life of the survivors will never be the same after they lose a loved one. Someone's spirit has left this earth and there will be rearranged holidays and empty chairs, bouts of anger and regret, and deep sorrow, along with profound memories and cherished legacy stories. Some survivors may be less energetic and a little bewildered. Others may shift right into planning mode, feeling the need to be productive, and start arranging the memorial or funeral service right in the deceased's room. "After all, everyone's here," this person might say. Be gentle with everyone who is part of the circle of love, including these type As who are only trying to help, and calmly reassure them there will be time to plan. Encourage everyone present to take in the moment. Be present and silent.

What Happens to the Body When a Person Dies?

If your loved one dies at home on hospice, a medical staff doctor or nurse practitioner will come to the residence soon after someone makes the call to the hospice's 24-hour line. If your loved one is in a hospital, a doctor from the care team will be called into the room. In both scenarios, the medical practitioner will perform the following tasks:

- Check vital signs (heartbeat, pulse, breathing).
- Check pupils for fixation and dilation.
- Check monitors in room, then turn them off.
- Declare a time of death, which will be noted in the death record and on the death certificate.

If you are the next of kin, you may be asked to confirm the identity of the deceased. The doctor may ask you or a family member if an autopsy (either partial or entire body) is desired. Performed generally within the first few days after the death, an autopsy is a comprehensive examination of a body to discover the cause of death or the extent of disease. Only a small fraction of deaths require an autopsy. Many families who have walked along with a patient's prolonged or chronic illness opt out of the autopsy as they are aware of all the procedures and processes that were done and how the death eventually occurred. However, with sudden deaths and unknown reasons, many families want to know what happened. An autopsy attempts to answer that question. Some types of death, such as those resulting from falls or fires must be reported to the local coroner. This varies depending on the locale and I discuss it in more detail in the next section of this chapter (see "The Death Report and Death Certificates" on pages 147–148). In coroner's cases, an autopsy will be performed.

Organ and Whole-Body Donation

It is likely, depending on the state you are in and/or hospital protocol, that the doctor or nurse will make a report to an organ donation agency. In the likelihood a person's organs are viable for donation, the organ donation agency will reach out to the family directly. There is no obligation to make a donation and the patient's illness determines whether their organs can be utilized. Please don't be offended if the agency cannot transplant your loved one's organs. For all sorts of reasons, transplantation simply isn't medically sound or reasonable. However, in some cases, a person's corneas or bones or skin may be a living grace to another. Simply be open to the possibility of donation if that is the wish of the deceased per their advance directive (see more about donation in chapter 3, "Talking about Health and Illness," starting on page 79 and chapter 4, "Putting Your House in Order," starting on page 95). It is the job of either the agent or proxy of the advance directive (if they are present) or the next of kin to make the decision about organ donation.

In the majority of cases, a whole-body donation to a medical school or research institution must be done in advance by application. To do this, an application is filed with the institution and, upon death, the institution decides if it is feasible to take the body for research. In most cases, cremation will take place after research, and the ashes will be returned to the family. However, this varies from institution to institution and should be discussed in advance. If the ashes can be returned, a family member will be notified when the cremains are available, usually several weeks later. Clearly a whole-body donation is a loving act of grace, and many may benefit from the generosity, but, as with organ donation, not everyone qualifies. Please discuss whole-body donation with your loved ones and make arrangements well in advance if at all possible.

The hospital will make their reports and inform those on the deceased's advance directive and members of the family noted in their chart. A hospital or facility typically allows the body of the deceased to remain in the room for a certain period of time (usually six–eight hours or less) so family members can come and pray, offer a ritual, or wait for others to gather so the inner circle can be together. You may wish to call the facility chaplain, if one is in the hospital, to assist you at this time. As I discussed in chapter 5, "Saying Goodbye and the Dying Process," on page 131, chaplains may be trained in multiple religious practices and may provide comfort to your family or facilitate finding the appropriate pastor, priest, imam, person to chant, reader, or spiritual practitioner.

Please be sure to notify the medical personnel in charge of the deceased of your wishes. If the death is a coroner's case, (see the next section, "What If Death Occurs at Home or Under Unusual Circumstances?") all members of the mourning group may not have the time to get to the hospital before the body is transferred to the medical examiner. When this happens, survivors will be informed that they can visit the deceased at the county morgue.

In most cases, the medical staff prepares the body for the cold room or morgue (unless this is counter to religious preferences, an autopsy is to be performed, or any of the special situations that are discussed in the rest of this chapter are in force. See bottom of this page through page 147.). Medical staff removes any apparatus, tubes, and external instruments, cleans the body, and places the body in a sanitized bag with identification. If an autopsy is to be performed, the body is transferred to the pathology department. If the body is to be released to a funeral home or cremation agency, the body is then taken to the facility morgue or cold room to await transport.

If the deceased did not do so before death, survivors may wish to select the crematorium, funeral home, or burial agency at the hospital, or survivors can wait until the family has all gathered to make a decision and call in their preference to the hospital's administrator. For a hospice patient, the decision regarding burial details has normally been made in advance. In that case, the hospice agency is in charge of removing the body from the home or nursing care center. In this situation, the deceased goes directly to the facility that will prepare the body for burial or cremation.

What If Death Occurs at Home or Under Unusual Circumstances?

If a death occurs at home or somewhere else other than a health care facility and the deceased is not on hospice, a county coroner will likely be involved. Someone needs to call the police at 911. The police will then verify and report the death. The county medical examiner team will come to the scene of the death to examine the body and check vital signs and the surroundings or place of death. The medical examiner's team may ask witnesses questions to determine how the death occurred. After their review, they remove the body to the county morgue. An autopsy is performed to discover the cause of death. Survivors may be allowed to view the deceased at the county offices. It is important to make arrangements well in advance with the county medical examiner's office to find an appropriate time to visit the county morgue, if allowed.

The following list includes some of the reasons a death may be designated a "coroner's case":

- Homicide or suicide
- Death due to injury or accident
- Death due to suspicious circumstances
- Death due to criminal activity
- Death in an institutional setting (prison, jail, or when a person is under control of a law enforcement agency)
- Death in the emergency room or operating room
- Death due to poisoning
- Unattended deaths
- Death of an unidentified person with no known next of kin
- Death of a person with no medical history
- Death at home when a person is not on hospice
- Death by a known or suspected contagious disease
- Death due to acute alcohol or drug intoxication

A death being a "coroner's case" does not necessarily mean a crime has been committed. It simply implies that there were no professional medical personnel present to witness or declare the nature of death. It could also reflect a lack of medical history or family, or an unexplained cause of death or sudden death during a procedure. The coroner analyzes the patient's medical condition, medical history, and circumstances at the time of death. If the coroner chooses not to take the body from a hospital, a referral number signifies that the coroner's office has reviewed the case and the body is released to the hospital's cold room or morgue.

Specific Religious Concerns and Preparations

For Hindu, Jewish, and Muslim families, there may be a 24-hour requirement to carry out specific burial practices. In these situations, the family of the deceased may request to bypass the cold room or morgue and ask for a direct transfer to a specific funeral home, crematorium, or memorial agency. This is done so specific preparations such as special washing, wrapping of the body, prayers, and other rituals can be carried out by the appropriate community members within the customary timeline. Most hospitals are prepared for such a request, but it's highly recommended the family call the specific funeral home or facility and ask the facility to inform the hospital of their plans and coordinate the process of transfer.

A body cannot be buried without a death certificate, and even the best-laid plans for burial can be complicated or delayed due to the difficulty of completing a death certificate in 24 hours. This is especially true on a holiday, on the weekend when offices are closed, or when limited staff is available. The hospital will try to honor specific requests as feasible.

Buddhist patients may request complete silence for many hours to days post-death. They may also request a direct transfer to a private home. This is done to allow the spirit to leave the body in peace. If a body is to be transferred to a private home, additional paperwork and permission will be required for the transport. Check with facility officials on how you can carry out these requests with as little disruption and stress for the survivors as possible. For more detailed information regarding specific religious requests, please refer to "Religious and Cultural Considerations" in the appendix on pages 221–234.

The Death Report and Death Certificates

Immediately after the death has been declared, a doctor enters a death summary into an electronic hospital reporting system or hospice file. Many of the facts of that death report eventually become part of the death certificate. A death certificate confirms the time, place, and cause(s) of death, in addition to other personal family information about the deceased.

Although the hospital, hospice, or care agency begins to generate the death certificate, survivors are not immediately issued a death certificate at the facility where the loved one died. The death certificate may take days or even weeks to complete. After the medical facility completes their portion of the form, the information is transferred to the family's choice of a funeral home, crematorium, or other agency. If a death is a coroner's case, the county will produce the certificate.

Survivors may be asked a lot of questions to help complete the form. These may include questions about the deceased's military service, mother's maiden name, social security number, birthplace and birthdate, and current address. People who need the certificates can ultimately order copies from whichever burial service finishes filling out the form. It is highly recommended that the people dealing with the estate order a minimum of 10 and up to 20 originals for all the banks, legal entities, and other professionals who will need them to settle the estate. Always keep at least two original copies for yourself. Some banks and institutions will accept a photocopy if you bring the original and allow them to make their copy in their establishment.

A Checklist for the Personal Representative

Here I provide a checklist of all the things that the person who deals with the estate of the deceased needs to take care of. It is a daunting list and it takes a strong person to complete. This is why it is important that any agent understands their duties before they sign up to be a personal representative. If you are a personal representative, agent, or proxy, you may want to delegate some of the tasks to other family members or friends. And by all means, ask questions and look to the experts if you are in over your head. The good news is, if the deceased collected the data listed in chapter 4, "Putting Your House in Order," it will be easier to start on this list. (Note that the term "decedent" refers to the person who has died.)

A Checklist for the Personal Representative

1. Notify the appropriate facility (hospice, funeral home, or donation agency) of the death.

2. As appropriate, notify clergy/officiant/leader of the decedent's faith community.

3. Arrange for care of any minor or elderly persons or pets dependent on the care provided by the decedent.

4. Check for written instructions regarding guidance for body disposition and funeral plans and make sure the wishes of the decedent are carried out. (See chapter 4, "Putting Your House in Order," page 89, for the list of the essential information and documents that should be gathered in one archive prior to death.)

5. Notify family members, employer, employees, and friends about the death.

6. Arrange for verification of death and arrange to receive an adequate number of death certificates. The funeral/cremation agency or donation agency provides these (see page 110).

7. Locate the original will of the decedent.

8. Notify personal representatives and any trustees named in the will if there are others besides you.

9. Collaborate with family to make arrangements for funeral/memorial services and carry out any predesignated wishes about the memorial the decedent has left in writing.

10. Prepare an obituary including the time and place of services. Include a list of appropriate memorials. Deliver obituary to the local paper.

11. Notify decedent's attorney, CPA, and insurance agents about the death.

12. Inquire into all benefits payable upon death such as Social Security, insurance, credit unions, and military. File claims as necessary.

13. Notify utility services, post office, landlord (if one is involved) about the death. Notify social media accounts. Monitor the decedent's mail carefully or have it automatically forwarded.

14. Retain an attorney and possibly an accountant to begin any necessary probate procedures and to provide general assistance.

15. Oversee and preserve the decedent's assets.

16. Locate any assets (including potentially hidden assets) and investigate all real property owned by the decedent.

17. If needed, arrange for out-of-state probate concerning any out-of-state real property.

18. Locate and obtain the contents of any safety deposit boxes.

19. Compile a detailed inventory of all assets. Check that this inventory corresponds to any list made by the decedent prior to death.

20. Notify specific financial institutions, financial advisors, and credit card companies as appropriate.

21. Determine proper values for all assets and be ready to support your valuations. An appraisal of all assets is strongly recommended.

22. Collect payment for all debts and, when appropriate, pay any outstanding debts of the decedent.

23. If necessary, decide which assets will be sold to pay the expenses of administration and taxes due because of death and arrange for such sales.

24. Investigate the amount and validity of all claims against the estate.

25. Arrange for the payment of income and all death tax liability, as the personal representative is held personally liable for these.

26. Maintain the estate's assets in good order and repair.

27. Operate, if specifically authorized to do so, any business of decedent.

28. Supervise the administration of the estate.

29. Process any necessary litigation by or against the estate.

30. Prepare the final estate accounting. Request and obtain a closing letter from the Internal Revenue Service before distributing assets to beneficiaries.

A word of warning to folks whose job it is to make order of the chaos that death can precipitate: People are generally their worst and their best at a funeral or time of death. Those who seemed reasonable may suddenly go off the deep end, and others whom you assumed would be emotionally undone, may be silent and nonresponsive. Old feuds or arguments that were settled long ago may reemerge, especially when money and property are involved. As a personal representative, you have the power to delegate and determine when people are not ready to enter into useful discussions. Work to be available to people, as many don't have the right words or know how to act in the face of death. Forgive errant behavior; don't focus or blame anyone for the weird and inappropriate things that they say.

Arrangements for Burial, Cremation, Ecoburial, Etc.

You may have heard stories about funeral directors. You know, about a fellow in a black suit with a grim face who lectures you about how to honor"your loved one with outrageous costly caskets and ceremonies and ladles on the guilt. This is simply not their role. But misunderstandings can occur when people are unprepared, vulnerable, and drowning in an ocean of grief. When you know the wishes of the deceased, this whole drama can be avoided. Hopefully, your loved one already let you know what they want. And if the "Body Disposition and Memorial Planning Worksheet" in the appendix on page 209 has been filled out, you will be miles ahead. Whether they chose a formal casket, cremation with a fancy urn, simple interment (the burial of a corpse in a grave or tomb, typically with funeral rites) at a public cemetery, interment at a celebrity funeral plot in Hollywood, a cardboard box of cremains scattered over a favorite beach or mountain, a green burial, composting, or to be buried alongside other family members, just be sure to take your list of requirements with you to meet with the representatives at the funeral home or crematorium.

The price range varies from an economical cremation at about $800–$1500, to mahogany caskets and processionals at celebrity burial grounds that can run thousands of dollars. This is why I advocate preplanning and not prepaying for the burial expenses, especially if the agency does not have reciprocity across state lines (see pages 95–96). It is so devastating for a family to find they have a prepaid plan that doesn't travel. It is such a gift to the family when the decedent has preplanned the arrangements, caskets, and plots, and set aside enough money to carry these wishes out.

As you make decisions and plan, be sure to have the facility or agency itemize the bill. The following lists are samples of potential line items for some common options:

Casket Burial/Interment at a Cemetery

- Transfer of body from the hospital or home to a mortuary/funeral home
- Casket
- Embalming
- Viewing at the funeral home
- Transfer of body to the ceremony
- Ceremony at the place of worship or funeral home's chapel
- Sound technicians or musicians to perform at the ceremony
- Plot or crypt
- Use of church/temple/mosque
- Transfer of casket to the place of burial
- Graveside ceremony and casket interment
- Officiant or person to perform the graveside ceremony
- Copies of death certificates

Cremation and Interment/Burial

- Transfer to cremation site
- Cremation
- Urn/container and engraving

- Ceremony at the place of worship or funeral home's chapel
- Musicians or technicians to perform at the ceremony
- Plot or crypt
- Us of church/temple/mosque
- Officiant or person to perform the graveside ceremony
- Copies of death certificates=

Cremation and Scattering

- Transfer to cremation site
- Cremation
- Container
- Ceremony at the place of worship or funeral home's chapel
- Musicians or technicians to perform at the ceremony
- Use of church/temple/mosque
- Cost of permits to deposit cremains in a specific location
- Possible boat or plane rental and pilot
- Copies of death certificates

And the following costs are common to most ceremonies as well:

- Flowers
- Additional officiant fees for each ceremony (for example, burial, interment or inurnment, and memorial)
- Reception, celebration, and meals
- Guest book

- Acknowledgment cards

- Cost of printing memorial program if not included in ceremony cost

Inurnment and Interment

The inurnment or interment refers to the ceremony in which the deceased is laid to rest. An inurnment is when cremains (the cremated remains in an urn) are laid in a cemetery, a crypt, a national burial site (see the next section "The US Department of Veterans Affairs" on page 156), or memorial wall. Interment is a casket or full-body burial. These ceremonies can take place in a variety of settings—a church memorial garden, a national burial site, a large private burial ground, public cemeteries, or cemeteries set aside for specific religions.

Some families find that it makes more sense to perform the ritual of burial before the memorial, as the burial is generally considered a more private and emotional time of good-byes. The inurnment or interment service itself is brief since most of the services take place at the burial site as people are standing under a canopy near the deceased's remains. Rituals of placing flowers on the casket or urn are often part of the ceremony as are sacred scriptures, poems, prayers, and short stories about the loved one. Generally, people ask the pastor, priest, or spiritual leader who leads the memorial to also perform inurnment or interment ceremonies. They can assist the family with the transition from graveside to the place of worship and provide a variety of readings for the different services. (Specific religious rites and ceremonies are covered in the "Religious and Cultural Considerations" section in the appendix on pages 221–234.)

The US Department of Veterans Affairs (VA)

The US Department of Veterans Affairs (VA) manages the largest multi-site burial grounds in the United States. If you are helping to arrange for the burial of a veteran, before you contact the VA for funeral or memorial arrangements, please have the following ready: legal name of deceased, honorable discharge papers (a DD214 document), ID card or serial number, military branch affiliation (navy, army, etc.), dates of service, social security number, and birth and death dates (a death certificate will suffice). It is also good to know if there is a history of other family members buried in a specific burial site.

The VA is equipped to provide the following as available: the date for burial (this can take months as many sites are full and waiting lists are common), the specific outdoor chapel or site where the service will take place, a military gun salute, the playing of taps, a flag ceremony and, as needed, a chaplain who can perform the brief service (typically 15–30 minutes).

After the service, the veteran will be buried or placed in a crypt or memorial wall, and the family can generally visit the place of burial later in the day. The family will receive documentation as to where the burial took place and a map to locate the site, in addition to the flag that was used in the ceremony.

These services are provided free of charge as a way to honor those who have served our country. The family's responsibility is to provide for the preparation of the body and find a way to transfer the casket or cremains to the military burial site. Chaplains affiliated with the site are available to perform the ceremony, but you may wish to have your faith leader perform the service around the military honors. For information regarding VA burial benefits can be found at https://www.va.gov/burials-memorials/.

Wakes

As family flies in from around the country, the evening before a memorial is often a time of gathering and remembering. The definition of the traditional Irish wake is "a watch held over a body of a dead person prior to burial and sometimes accompanied by festivity."[21] In modern times, the festivity part has taken over and the body has left the building; it is either already in the ground or waiting to be buried. Sometimes this kind of gathering will occur after a viewing at the mortuary or funeral home. Most people conceive of a wake as a time of partying, storytelling, and reminiscing. As a pastor, I love being invited to these gatherings, as it's the time when everyone lets their hair down and tells the truth. Most of the stories I hear never make the pulpit, but often this is a time to speak openly about a person's legacy and family devotion, and for the family to process some of its grief. I encourage such a time. It's a time to laugh and prepare for the deep emotional valleys you and your family are about to cross. It also provides a time for the family to check in about last-minute details of the day to come—the memorial or celebration of life. In the Roman Catholic tradition, the wake is also known as the Rosary, and it is a service held the day before the funeral mass, normally in the location of worship of the deceased or at the funeral home. The tradition began as a vigil in Celtic times to "hold a wake over" a corpse and protect it from evil spirits. Now it is a service of prayers, tributes, and remembrance.

Memorials and Tributes

If the decedent filled out the "Body Disposition and Memorial Planning" and "Eulogy and Obituary Planning" worksheets in the appendix when they completed their archive in chapter 4, many of the preferences for the memorial may already be addressed or even preplanned. For those who have not had a chance to preplan, the following information will help shape the memorial and/or funeral service.

For most people, the time after a loved one dies is a sacred time of remembrance. The majority of services take place in a house of worship but, for the sake of time and proximity, many may be performed at the funeral home near the burial site. Typically, services are presided over by the spiritual leader of the deceased's religion or affinity group and last about 45 minutes to an hour in length. Those who wish to include additional speakers, music, and slideshows can extend the service to last the better part of an hour and a half or two hours. Not all services have programs, but it is helpful to create one if you want to have the audience participate and know the order of the service or what to say or sing. Appoint a person early on to handle the format and printing based on your wishes. Many places of worship have administrators who handle the layout and printing of the program for the memorial.

It is highly recommended that you read through "Religious and Cultural Considerations: in the appendix on pages 221–234 as well. For many religions, however, memorial services have the following common components:

- Opening greeting and words of comfort
- Reading of prayers, sacred text, or scripture
- Music (hymns, vocal soloists, or instrumentalists)
- Eulogy (A eulogy is a speech that praises someone or something highly, typically someone who has just died. This is the story of a person's life and it can also be printed in the memorial program.)

- Specific rituals (for example, those involving flame, water, earth, or sacred artifacts)

- A meditation (for example, a meaningful brief talk about the sacred texts and the life of the person usually given by the person in charge of service)

- Speakers or people who provide testimonials on the impact of a person's life on them or humanity

- Slideshow (I generally suggest people hold off on this for the reception.)

- Dedication of the soul

- Closing thoughts and benediction

Note that it is up to the specific house of worship if they will allow the cremains or casket to be displayed. Always check first. Each religion has its own set of rules for these services.

Making It Personal

Most religious or faith leaders are grateful if the family comes up with sacred texts and music in advance. If the family has, they can weave the service around those personal choices. This may take some digging. Not everyone has a bedside Bible, sacred text, or book of favorite poems lying around in the open. However, if your loved one does and you are able to find it, you usually have some clues as to the texts that matter to the deceased. Look for highlights, dog-eared pages, or bookmarks.

The other essential task for survivors is to talk and write down character qualities and share those insights with the person in charge of the ceremony. This helps that person to personalize the story they tell at the memorial. Nothing is more aggravating than a service featuring generalized platitudes that have nothing to do with the deceased.

Give a complete portrait of the person to the person who will lead the memorial so that the people attending the memorial learn something new. If the deceased has already prepared a eulogy for the service or obituary for the newspaper, you can present those to the officiant. Or you may wish to use the written autobiography or story the deceased has prepared as part of chapter 2, "Making Wishes Known to Loved Ones" (see pages 50–54). If your loved one has left you no clear indication of their wishes, the following outline may prove helpful.

To help give the memorial a personal and meaningful impact, try to answer the following questions about your loved one:

- What was their family like during the growing up years? Were they loving? Was Dad or Mom in the military and absent? Did they enjoy family time and vacations together? What was school like?

- What was their passion in life? What was their dream and did they accomplish it? Did they have an ambition to become an astronaut or inventor? A famous entertainer or athlete?

- Whom did they mentor, love, engage with? How did they make a difference? Who were the people impacted by their life? What event or accomplishment were they most proud of?

- What was their impact on their children, family, and friends, and what were the things that mattered to them? How did they influence their children to achieve what they did? What was their marriage like?

- Did they visit exotic places? Did they scale Everest?

- Where they an artist and created something amazing?

- Did their humble beginnings inspire them to work hard and achieve the impossible? Did they overcome insurmountable obstacles and use their setbacks as lessons for life?

- Did their faith or religion impact their life? Did their faith play a part in their accomplishments or difficulties? Did they participate in philanthropic or mission work?

Who Should Speak?

I generally ask a family to choose three speakers: one to tell the personal story about the growing up and formative years (a sibling or childhood friend is a good candidate to handle this); one to talk about the loved one's integrity, leadership and impact on the world (for this, you might choose a fellow volunteer, a business associate, or coworker); and one to get at the core of the deceased's personality. This last speaker might be a best friend. It can be the person who knew the deceased inside out in good times and bad times. Look for a friend who can tell a lot of great anecdotes about the deceased and their friendship. Three speakers can usually touch on the full spectrum of the personality.

I don't suggest or expect members of the family to speak unless someone insists. It's simply too emotional a time. If a close family member really wants to, it is helpful if they write out what they want to say before the memorial. That way if they are overwhelmed, someone else (usually the person presiding) can step in and read their tribute for them.

I often suggest that grandchildren or extended family members read the sacred texts or poems as this role doesn't require a lot of preparation and this is a good way to make them feel part of the service. More mature grandchildren can be a great addition to the speaker list as they can tell the truth well and usually offer fun stories.

You may be the one asked to write a memorial tribute. And in a time of shock and loss, that can be difficult. But think of the things you remember. Write out five short stories that remind you of the person and how they touched you or touched others. Was there a time they had your back and stood up for you? Were there things they taught you that had lasting significance? Did you have a challenge or need that they met, not expecting anything in return? What were their gifts, the things they did naturally, and how did they contribute to a better world? Still pondering? Check out the Cake website https://www.joincake.com/blog/tribute-speech/ for more ideas.

Most importantly, ask the speakers to keep their contributions short. They should be three to five minutes long at a maximum. Music, anecdotes, personal insights, and pictures are wonderful pieces in the program, but if things slow down and run long, it can be hard on the family. A slideshow later at the reception can fill in some of the blanks and provide pictures to round out the story.

I am in favor of eliminating the open mic part of the program as it can be an unpleasant surprise if someone decides to tell the "real story" about how "Mary" was a wild party animal dancing on tables and drinking her way through college. (Yes, I have seen this sort of thing actually happen!)

A Wonderful Discussion and a Wonderful Send-Off

One of the most intimate and special times for me was discussing the scriptures and music my sister-in-law wanted for her service before she died. It took her a long time to agree to talk about it, but once she knew her time was limited and recovery was not in the picture, the information flowed from her. The service was exactly as she requested: simply glorious. It was full of great music, scripture, and memories from her sister, Anne, about growing up together, tearful memories from my brother, David, about their courtship and her stellar faith, a few words from a friend, Vicky, who was a warrior for special needs children including her son, Jeremy (who also spoke), her nephew (our son) Floyd's poignant vocal solo, stirring hymns, and praise songs, and on the organ, Vidor's "Toccata" at full stop to end it all. It was the perfect send-off because she knew what she wanted in advance and communicated that.

Other Considerations at a Memorial

Whether there are pictures, guest books, and things like that at the memorial is obviously all up to the family. Many families choose to have a few pictures in a room of the worship center, chapel, or family home along with a guest book. In the past, mourners would send elaborate gifts of bouquets and arrangements to the funeral home or worship site. This is no longer the case, as modern sensibilities tell us to avoid waste. Instead, the family or extended family normally provide the flowers for the service and reception (often used for both events) with the deceased in mind. Did they love roses? Daisies? Peonies? Is there any particular color they were fond of?

In lieu of expecting folks to purchase and send flowers, some families list a favorite charity of the deceased in the obituary and memorial program. If the deceased had a particular passion for animals, perhaps the Humane Society would be appropriate, or if they loved flowers, a garden society may be better. Some families ask that donations be given to a house of worship or to a mission or philanthropic charity that the deceased cared about. In any case, submit your ideas and appropriate addresses and websites to the person in charge of creating the program for the memorial service.

One last thing. You may wish to have someone at the deceased's home during the service if the date and time are listed in the newspaper or online source. Sadly, there are those who would commit a robbery during this time and the home needs to be protected.

The Reception

Most guests at a service expect a place to have tea or coffee and a chance to offer their condolences to the family. They also might want to share a few additional stories with friends. This is a wonderful place to have a PowerPoint slideshow and a photo gallery of the person's life.

The reception generally follows the memorial or celebration service on the same site. Your worship facility may offer a simple reception as part of their services. Be sure you ask if this is included in the fee or additional expenses are expected. If you plan to have extra food, cater it and make sure there are people to clean up or wrap up the leftovers.

For more intimate situations, the family may choose to have this reception at a private home or restaurant. Please make this clear in the memorial program and provide a map or way to get there.

A Reception to Remember

If you have the energy to do so, it is nice to be creative and personal in planning a reception. We've already mentioned choosing colors of flowers and memorial donations to charitable organizations, but here are some additional ways to celebrate:

- Serve a favorite snack or dessert of the deceased's at the reception and include the recipe.

- In the picture display at the reception, make collages that depict specific portions of that person's life with topics like "family," "workplace and accomplishments," "vacations," "military service," etc.

- Display artifacts, awards, certificates, and other points of honor along with hats, buttons, and trophies.

- Have fun with the slideshow and include a few pictures featuring costumes, fun times, and kids and their antics.

- If you have a live recording of their voice, that's fun to add.

- Don't forget the music. If they loved the Beatles, opera, jazz, or soul, play it loud.

What Happens If It Is Not Possible to Plan an In-Person Funeral or Memorial?

The recent pandemic has forced us into a world of virtual good-byes, solo grieving, and a sense of profound isolation without a community to honor the dead. Survivors may feel depressed, full of guilt, or anxious simply because they didn't have the opportunity to provide a loving tribute to a lost loved one. Fortunately, there are some resources available to begin the grieving process and offer some closure.

Consider the following suggestions by Dr. Shoshana Ungerleider:

- Create an online memorial scrapbook. Lifeweb360 (https://www.lifeweb360.com/) offers an online experience for families and friends to celebrate and remember the life of their loved ones by sharing videos, stories, letters, and photos online for everyone to experience.

- Have a virtual funeral. Visit GatheringUs (https://www .gatheringus.com/) to use their online platform to create a personalized virtual funeral or ceremony. LifeWeb 360 teamed up with NewNarrative to offer a free, online guide to create virtual end of life events (https://www.newnarrative.ca/covid19).

- Attend an online candlelight vigil. Reimagine (https:// www.letsreimagine.org/) is hosting monthly virtual candlelight vigils to honor the memory of those who have died with COVID-19.[22]

Think about what people would want to experience if they cannot be there and attend on Zoom. Can you provide a way for someone to speak to the family if they are online during the ceremony? What kind of interactive things can be added to the ceremony? In short, you can still do your best to honor the person in a way they would love. Tell their story joyfully so people will remember them. Celebrate their life with meaningful cultural and religious traditions, mourn the loss, and visually document their legacy.

7

Piecing Things Back Together after Death: Conversations around Grief and Loss

You will lose someone you can't live without, and your heart will be badly broken, and the bad news is that you never completely get over the loss of your beloved. But this is also the good news. They live forever in your broken heart that doesn't seal back up. And you come through. It's like having a broken leg that never heals perfectly—that still hurts when the weather gets cold, but you learn to dance with the limp.

—Anne Lamott

No one ever told me that grief felt so like fear.

—C. S. Lewis

Grief and loss are a shared tale.

—Jason Rosenthal

The human soul doesn't want to be advised or fixed or saved. It simply wants to be witnessed exactly where it is.

—Parker Palmer

Sukla

Sukla laid out her husband's clothes on the bed. It had been nearly a month since his death, and she was beginning to clean the closets and do the downsizing necessary to move in with her son and daughter-in-law. She was beginning the new chapter in her life as a widow. Before her lay his opulent ceremonial shirts with gold threads alongside the simple cotton T-shirts he wore while weeding the garden. There was the coat he was married in and the turban he wore to his granddaughter's party, a colorful scarf with batik design for the Holi festival, and some pants made of the finest silk for Diwali, the festival of light. Sukla sat there for what seemed like the entire afternoon, running her hands across the fabrics, each a distinct landscape, smelling each one. She began to think about a way she could preserve these precious memories. Remembering the soft warm blankets of her childhood, she cut a square from each of these pieces of clothing and decided to piece together a memory quilt. She would wrap herself up in his warm embrace each night as she went to bed and remember the man who still breathed life into each square. And when her grandchildren pointed to a square, the stories embedded in the blanket would come to life.

Mohammed

Mohammed, or Sonny as his parents called him, was one of our son's best friends. Sadly, Sonny lost his sister, Sonja, to a careless driver who hit and killed her one night while she was trying to rescue a dog in the middle of the street. Sonny's parents were devastated, and relatives flew in from the Middle East and all parts of the country to mourn her tragic death. Her family followed their custom of washing and wrapping the body for the burial, an extended period of mourning, interment, the traditional Muslim memorial, and more mourning and wailing for their precious daughter for a total of 40 days. As the intensity of the sadness would be difficult for an 11-year-old, Sonny stayed with our family during this time. Once the mourning period was over, Sonny returned home to reunite with his parents. But Sonja's room was untouched and would remain so for many months; so grieved by her death, her parents wanted to retain her memory.

Your Chapter 7 Checklist:

1. Learn about well-known models of grieving and loss and how they may be able to help you.

2. Benefit from the author's experience from her ten general principles on grief and loss (pages 176–193).

3. Find professionals and other resources to help you and others successfully grieve and find meaning in death.

There are no simple explanations for grief and loss. Survivors often feel disoriented and disappointed. In our attempt to realign our lives, we try to locate lost pieces, while the rest of the world seems to go on uninterrupted. But often we come up short, and the unpredictable mood swings and emotional upheaval leave us feeling empty and alone because no one gets it.

This chapter is about ways you can work through the loss. Initially, I recommend that you take some time to just be—to assess where you are, to do less for a while. One way to begin is by scanning through the coming months and plan time for some specific tasks of grieving, things you need to do as you struggle to find the new normal without your loved one in your life. As I will say countless times, there are no perfect timelines. You set the schedule.

Models of Grieving

Although there are countless models for working through grief, in this chapter I discuss three popular models and the authors who developed them: the four tasks of mourning of William Worden, the five stages of grief of Elizabeth Kübler-Ross, and the four stages of grief of John Bowlby. Grief is a personal process and one of these lists of stages or tasks may work for you while others may not. You may even wish to cherry-pick parts of all three to work through your time of mourning. Decide which works best for you, and by all means read one or all three of the authors' books to get a comprehensive view of their theories.

William Worden's Four Tasks of Mourning

In his book *Grief Counseling and Grief Therapy: A Handbook for the Mental Health Practitioner*, Fifth Edition, psychologist William Worden describes the four tasks of healthy mourning that he first described in the 1980s as those things "one must accomplish for the process of mourning to be completed" and "equilibrium to be established."[23]

The first task, accepting the reality of the loss, involves going through the ritual of the memorial or funeral, beginning to speak about the person in the past tense, and accepting the way they died. Many people are in denial about the reality of death, but until it is fully accepted, it's hard to move on and reestablish your life. Note that in accomplishing this task, suicide, an overdose, or another stigmatized death may present additional challenges to family and friends in contrast to a natural or expected death.

The second task is processing the pain of grief. Worden acknowledges that each person and each loss will involve working through a range of different emotions including sadness, fear, loneliness, despair, hopelessness, anger, guilt, blame, shame, relief, and others. An obstacle to accomplishing this important task is that some people wish to deny the feelings or skip them altogether. Most people, especially those who have not gone through the mourning process themselves, experience discomfort hearing about these emotions as well. You may not be the life of the party for a while. Allow yourself to feel these difficult emotions and to process the feelings with a trusted friend, mentor, or family member.

The third task is adjusting to a world without the deceased. This happens over an extended period of time and involves internal and external adjustments. Sometimes, we may not recognize the roles that people played in our lives until a person no longer functions in that environment. Or you may miss the things that a person did for you, such as taking care of the day-to-day maintenance of your shared home, maintaining your social calendar, or orchestrating the daily events of your family life. For example, if you lost a co-parent, you have to learn to accept that while once there were two of you managing the children, school, after-school sports, and weekend activities, your co-pilot is now gone. Who will handle that role? What provisions must be put in place to keep things running smoothly without them? After a person dies, we have to adjust and adapt to the new normal in order to keep moving forward and not get stuck.

The last of Worden's four tasks is finding an enduring connection with the deceased in the midst of embarking on a new life. This involves emotionally relocating the deceased and moving on with life. We must find an appropriate, ongoing connection in our emotional lives with the person who has died that still allows us to continue living. As you accomplish this task, you continue to think of your missing loved one and cherish memories, but you also begin to meaningfully engage in things that bring pleasure, new things, or new relationships.

Elizabeth Kübler-Ross's Five Stages of Grief

Swiss-American psychiatrist Elizabeth Kübler-Ross was a pioneer in encouraging people to talk about the once a taboo subject of death. Inspired by her work with terminally ill patients, her 1960 book, *On Death and Dying: What the Dying Have to Teach Doctors, Nurses, Clergy, and Their Own Families*,[24] gave people permission to do the work of grieving. This section of the chapter is a brief summary of the Kübler-Ross stages of grief, which are experienced by terminally ill patients prior to death as well as people who have lost a loved one. The five stages are: denial, anger, bargaining, depression, and acceptance.

During the initial stage of denial, the world becomes meaningless and overwhelming. Life makes no sense. In this stage, you may believe the diagnosis is somehow mistaken and that you won't die. A survivor may be in shock and go numb and wonder how they can "go on." This stage allows those who are grieving to cope and make survival possible. It can help us to pace our feelings of grief and help let in only as much as we can handle.

The second stage, anger, is also necessary for the healing process. Even though there is some stigma against expressing these feelings, the more a person truly feels the anger, the more it will begin to dissipate and healing can begin. Anger has no limits and can be focused on inner circles of friends and families, and/or toward outer circles of religion and God. Underneath all the anger is pain, and it's a natural at this time to question God and to feel deserted and abandoned. See anger as a temporary structure for the nothingness of the loss. Anger is a gauge of the intensity of your feelings and your love.

When you are in the bargaining stage, you may find yourself thinking, "Please, God, I will never be angry again if you will just let them live." Your negotiation for your own or a loved one's extended life is made in exchange for change in your lifestyle. This sort of deal-making is common during this stage. "If only" scenarios begin to take over your thought processes. Guilt becomes a bargainer's companion. The "if only" process can make you to find fault in yourself and you may become fixated on what you could have done differently. You simply don't want to feel the pain of the loss and try to negotiate your way out of the hurt.

Depression often follows bargaining. When you realize death is inevitable and the negotiations are done, you move from the fantasy world of what could be to the reality. Your grief reaches a deeper level. Unlike the brief negotiation dialogues, this stage may feel like it could last forever. Situational depression is a common response to a great loss. You might retreat from life for a while in an intense fog of sadness. You may lose your motivation to accomplish tasks, wondering if you even have the will to live. This is a normal. When the loss truly becomes real and you face the realization that your loved one didn't get better this time and is not coming back, depression is a natural response.

Acceptance is the final of the Kübler-Ross stages. This stage is about accepting the reality that your loved one is physically gone and recognizing that this new reality is permanent. You may not like this reality, but you are learning to live with it. Your loved one is missing, and you now inhabit a modified world. You readjust or reorganize roles, reassign tasks, and realign your thinking. Although you can never replace the loss, you find yourself forming new connections, new relationships, and new interdependencies. You begin to listen to your needs and grow. You begin to invest in friendships and make a greater investment in yourself. In short, you begin to live again.

An additional stage, meaning, was added by Kübler-Ross' co-author David Kessler after her death. Kessler notes that finding meaning beyond grief involves moving forward in a way that honors loved ones and transforms grief into a hopeful experience. In this stage, a person begins to discover things that inspire them to focus on new hopes and dreams.

John Bowlby's Four Stages of Grief

British psychologist and psychiatrist John Bowlby's stages of grief begin with seeing death as a loss (of a significant person, of a job or home, or of an old stage of life). After death, the stages of grieving begin.

Shock and numbness is the stage that involves the emotions of dullness, denial, outbursts, and weight loss. You may not believe that your loss is real, and you may be in denial and unable or unwilling to accept your loss. Getting through this phase is necessary to process the loss we experience. This stage is also the gateway phase into the process of yearning, searching, and depression.

Yearning and searching occurs when we finally accept the reality of loss. This phase entails feelings of anger and guilt, and preoccupation with the deceased and what was lost. Manifestations of depression can result in crying, nausea, loss of appetite, irritability, self-criticism, and disturbed sleep.

Despair and disorientation is the next stage. It may seem as though life will never improve or make sense again without our deceased loved one. This is the stage characterized by confusion, apathy, withdrawal, restlessness, aimlessness, and feelings of unreality, decreased socialization, loneliness, and a sense of exile. But this is also a time where one can be patient, receptive, while waiting for the next chapter of life to begin.

In the stage of reorganization and recovery, finally we make attempts at new patterns of behavior and begin to find meaning in loss and death and a new life. Survivors accept the loss and find new interests and skills. Some may also experience a new or renewed socialization. Recovery signals a rebirth to a new form of life, a resurrection event.

Ten General Principles on Grief and Loss

The three formal models from mental health professionals described in the last section provide a general idea of the kinds of things to expect in the grieving process. However, you will probably not find all your answers there. It's likely you will be forging your own personal path to emotional health and taking much needed time to readjust. In my years as a pastor and chaplain, there are some general principles I have found to be true for many people who go through the grieving process. In the following material, I discuss these briefly.

1. There Is No Timeline: Grief Is Not Linear

It's disconcerting when people set a timeline for another person's grief. How many times have you heard words to this effect: "Oh, it's been a year, Fred. You can move on now."? This certainly may not be the case if Fred celebrated his sixtieth wedding anniversary with his now deceased wife. It also may not apply if the motorcycle accident involved a 19-year-old who was killed by a drunk driver. Setting a timeline and putting an expiration date on grief is ridiculous and unfair to the grieving person. Instead, the best thing community members can do for a grieving person is to check in regularly, be present and gentle, and affirm their efforts throughout the mourning process. To rely on a calendar to set deadlines is perilous, even cruel. Normally, the anniversary of a death is often the toughest day of the year, along with holidays, birthdays, wedding anniversaries, graduations, and other special occasions. So whether you are suffering the loss of a loved one or you are caring for someone else who is a survivor, be kind. Recognize the hurt, affirm the pain, and continue to celebrate the memory.

Grief does not pay attention to the calendar, nor is grief linear. Many people would like to follow a set formula. When they are "finished" with one stage of grieving or task of mourning, they would like to automatically move to the next. But grief has a wicked streak, and it can change its progress and pattern without notice. You may feel as though you are working toward Bowlby's reorganization phase or Kübler-Ross's acceptance phase (see pages 172–175) but then rage erupts from seemingly nowhere or denial rears its ugly head on an anniversary. Be prepared for aftershocks and unpredictable episodes in your grieving process. It's necessary that the stages be addressed and lived through, but you may not necessarily progress through the stages in order. Like trying to push a beach ball underwater, repressing or ignoring the stages only prolongs the process of healing. Eventually, the emotional stage you skipped bounces back to the surface to remind you that you're not done with your journey.

For some reason, our culture sets up the expectation that you can bounce back after a bereavement time of three days or a week and dive right back into work as if nothing happened. The problem with this expectation is it doesn't take into account the fact that your personhood has just taken a hit—and not just any hit, but a hit of epic proportions. Your emotional landscape is going to be in ruins for a while until the cleanup and rebuilding can begin.

Life is just not the same after you lose a loved one. It is not the same job, home, family gathering, or friendship. The empty chair, the missing place setting at the table, the unfilled seat in a car are striking reminders. As the various stages of grief take over, they color your attitude, activities, and focused time. You may feel exhausted and can't get the work done you used to do. Or you may find that relationships and the activities that filled your schedule don't bring joy or meaning anymore. It is okay to feel this way.

A challenging aspect of life for many is the workplace, which normally requires focus and productivity. You may feel like dropping out of life and your work. Take the time to talk to your employer and make temporary adjustments. More often than not, they will be compassionate and don't want to lose a valuable employee, so they will work with you.

If you are still working, taking a week off helps, especially when there are hundreds of details to attend to: chasing down the death certificate information, planning burial arrangements, and creating the inventory of things to manage, including bills, etc. But a few days off from work doesn't ease the deep sadness and loss. To believe life will go on and be the same is ludicrous.

If you need to, have a talk with your supervisor and let them know the extent of how this loss has affected you. Talk over what can be done to adjust your workload. Some supervisors are ahead of the curve and can assess what their needs are, what your capabilities are, and determine what can be set aside while you take some time off. You may have to rearrange your schedule, run meetings from home, and delegate certain tasks to an associate. This is to be expected and should be honored. If your workplace will not assist you, do the best you can. Take breaks or short walks during the day to calm your emotions. Excuse yourself during tender moments. Work on your mourning tasks on weekends, holidays, and days off. You may need to use your PTO (paid time off) or vacation to do the more intense grieving.

If you are now a widower or widow, one of the hardest parts of grieving is being solo. The dinner parties and couples' times are now a little unsettling. Fortunately, in the twenty-first century, this is not as much a problem as it used to be. With the trends toward group activities and less emphasis on traditional couples, hopefully your singleness won't prove to be a problem in your social circle. You have the right to tell someone you don't wish to be "fixed up" with another person and will be happy to attend events alone.

Mourning is also very difficult in families with children. If you have suffered the loss of a child, other families may find it hard to include you in social outings with children who knew your loved one. Decide how you will move forward and make choices that feel emotionally stable. You set the timeline and the scenarios.

Sometimes the grief is more than you can bear, and you can't find any meaning in your life. Or you may even feel completely adrift and want to end it all. You don't believe anyone would miss you and you are so miserable that you can't see any reason to live. If you are considering harming yourself, call someone right away to help you—a crisis hotline, suicide prevention hotline, or a trusted friend. Let them know how you are feeling and get help. Please reach out to someone immediately. It's not uncommon to feel this way, and you can work through the issues without harming yourself or anyone else. I've listed help lines here:

Crisis Text Line: Text HOME to 741-741

Disaster Distress Helpline: 1-800-985-5990

National Suicide Hotline: 1-800-273-8255 (273-TALK)

Veterans Crisis Line: 1-800-273-8255, then press 1

2. Know Who Your Friends Are

I encourage people to make sure that they have at least two "2:00 a.m. people" in their lives (see chapter 1, "Exploring and Expressing Meaning and Purpose, page 14). These are the friends who pick up the phone and listen with open hearts when you call them at 2 a.m. These are the friends who get you and get it. These are also the friends who are willing to sit with you and hear the story even if the story is sad or features resentment or regrets.

If you don't have people like this in your life, it's probably time to seek a professional therapist or a counselor who makes you feel safe when you share the tough stuff. A counselor is a gift we give ourselves. They have the power to reach deep inside of us and equip us with tools that will strengthen us. It is a sign of strength to ask for help.

Know that being "cheered up" doesn't work. Acknowledge where you are and do not let people try to bully you into acting happier than you feel or attempting to "fix" you. No one can take another person's pain away. It is the job of friends and family to let mourning people be "in it" and to stay near them. You are driving your own bus. Don't allow others to take the wheel.

Words That Don't Help

There are, of course, those who are well-meaning but say exactly the wrong thing. For instance, some might say, "It was meant to be; he suffered such a long time," "God must have needed her in heaven, she was such a good person," "Oh, don't worry, most people get over it and move on in a few months," "Time heals all wounds," or "Just work it through, get your mind off it. You'll be okay." When you hear platitudes like these, feel free to ignore the comment or politely walk away.

It is likely people who offer these "words of wisdom" are working from their own experience of loss, which may be little to none, or they simply don't have the emotional intelligence or any script to work from. After a long silence, a response might be, "I appreciate that you are thinking of me and appreciate your prayers and good wishes. I've got a lot of things to work through right now and I miss my loved one very much. I'll be sure to reach out and let you know when I want to talk about it." This both sets a boundary and begins the process of establishing the priorities of things that need to be accomplished and those that can be set aside for another time.

3. There Is No Right Way to Grieve

As I have already noted, there is no right way to work through a loss. Each person has their own personal path that may or may not include the various stages of grieving as laid out by the professionals we discussed in the previous section. You will most certainly experience some moments that are visceral and deep. This is your own journey and you have the right to map it out. Making decisions about when to clean out a loved one's possessions and when to restart a social life are personal. In general, it is better to move slowly than too quickly.

Doing things such as cleaning out a loved one's possessions should be on your terms and your timeline. Keeping loved one's possessions in their place is not a detriment to healing. In fact, one of the most healing times is when you can slowly move through the closet as Sukla does in the chapter-opening story. Take in the smells, savor the memories and special occasions. Rejoice in how the clothes, special collections, toys, or trinkets were a part of your loved one's life. This is not a time to be coerced, rushed, or pressured. Unless you are up against a deadline, take your time. Allow your feelings to sort the things to retain and the things that are no longer of value. For example, when my mother died a year after my dad, there were numerous things to sort and pack up. My sisters and I chose to take the weekend off. We put on some great '60s and '70s groove music, laughed, told stories, tried on our mother's wild outfits, including the leopard print pants and kilts, and sifted through the cookbooks. It was healing for all of us.

When you go through a loved one's possessions, you may want to take some individual or personal time or have a friend join you for a second opinion. This is a time of healing. Decide where possessions might go to honor the deceased. Have a garage sale or estate sale and give the money or leftover furnishings to a special charity, a philanthropic cause, or put the moneytoward tuition for college for a child, grandchild, or loved one. Perhaps a family relocation center for the homeless or disenfranchised would be the preferred choice. The possibilities are endless.

When you are grieving, it is a good idea to be vigilant about avoiding self-medication and poor lifestyle choices. With loss, there is an inevitable period of depression. Often with depression and lack of energy, you may feel the need to self-medicate with alcohol or drugs, make poor social or dating choices, or simply drop out of your life. This is where accountability and partnership come in. It might be helpful for you to have a daily or weekly check-in with a buddy (a trusted friend, mentor, or counselor) to hold you accountable and check in about goals, small accomplishments, or changes. They might also be able to get you out of the house and enjoy a meal or some entertainment as your mood and the budget allows. A change of venue and some variety in activities can help in the tough, deeply hurtful times. A counselor and/or a support group can help you set a course for what works best for you and find kindred souls who understand what you're going through.

Although each of us must make our own decisions about such things, dating may not be recommended for a while. I know people who join grief support groups in order to find a future mate, date them, and six months later are walking down the aisle. When someone has lost a mate or partner due to death or divorce, it's common to want to be near people for comfort and companionship. Our neediness often screams for attention of any kind. When you receive affection, touch, or affirmation, it feels very good. However, when the emotional tsunami hits your brain, why would you settle for a temporary shelter of quick emotional fixes when you could have a permanent dwelling of appropriate life giving relationships?

Grief and loss take time. Take time to clean up the debris of loss, truck out the anger, resentment, and depression, and rebuild into a new normal. Once you have done the hard work of grieving, there will be more of you to dedicate to a relationship. Grief takes up a lot of real estate in the brain. Sadly, many rebound romances end in nasty divorces, and the grief, sadness, and anger trigger the now compounded loss all over again. Friends, family gatherings, buddies, fellowship or affinity, and support groups can fill in this gap better than a new romance can.

4. Honesty Is the Best Policy

Be honest with people. There's no need to hide bad feelings, sadness, or grief. This is a good time to express to others what you need and what you want. As you go through the stages of grief, you will feel the full range of emotions. There is no way to go around them, so you must go through them.

Grieving My Father

It took a great deal of time for me to grieve the loss of my dad. I can remember sitting in my dining room about three months after my father died. My husband came up from behind attempting to hug me and I just came unglued. I didn't realize it at the time, but I felt intense anger and my husband's touch triggered all the deep sadness I was feeling. My response was "Don't touch me! I'm hurting!" and I burst into tears. For some reason, that Saturday I felt a flood of memories of my dad's immense compassion and wisdom and I was experiencing all my loss all at once. Stunned, my husband backed off and I told him I just couldn't respond or feel at that moment. I was honest and Frank got it. He walked away and let me have my space. By dinner, I could breathe again and process where my head was. Frank knew when to back off and didn't take it personally.

Those who try to comfort you might not know what to say, and that's okay. But you should be honest with them about what you do and do not need during this time. You might want to tell them that you'd like to talk about your deceased loved one even if it makes you sad. You might also need to tell them that the grief process may seem long, but wishing the grief away or ignoring it won't speed the process up. And ask people not to exclude you from events even if you don't feel like going. Letting people know how you feel, even if it's uncomfortable for you and for them, is better than making a difficult situation even worse through miscommunication.

You might try writing a letter to the deceased that describes your grief. Speak about how you miss your loved one and what it feels like. Tell them about their qualities that touched you and how their absence has altered your life. Declare your anger for things that didn't turn out as expected and how you miss the daily routines and special occasions. Let them know what you are doing to honor their legacy and work through the loss. Date the letter and put it away in a safe place for reference. For more information on writing these letters, The Center for Growth (www.therapyinphiladelphia.com) offers a resource called "Processing Grief through Writing Letters."

Once you have completed that letter, use those memories to compose a narrative to friends. I've found countless people detest getting holiday correspondence from people who don't know a loved one has died. Get ahead of the curve. Write a letter to family and friends who may want to know what happened and how you are coping. Inform them about the things that would be helpful to know or say to you and when you'll be ready to re-emerge for social gatherings or receive help with practical issues. This allows you some breathing room and sets boundaries around what you can handle.

5. You Can't Do It All: Delegating and Letting Go

"Many hands make light work," as my mother would say. Fortunately, I believed her. When the tasks of grieving were overwhelming, I knew to check in with friends and ask for help.

Grieving My Mother

The year my mother died, one year after my father's death, I was in an emotional fog. My family was hundreds of miles away, and my husband had to temporarily move for a new job, as he couldn't find work where we lived. I was left in an enormous empty house for over seven months to grieve on my own. Feeling abandoned and utterly alone, my mental health started to deteriorate. Deferred projects were left undone and the yard grew overgrown and brown in the scorching heat of summer. Swirling around in my emotional cocktail was fear. I felt fear that I wasn't strong enough or worthy of other's help. I felt as though I couldn't tell my friends or my covenant sisters (members of my women's ministry organization) about my absentee husband or the emotional cost of losing two parents in a span of 13 months. Someone got wind of my situation, however, and called me. "Tell us what you need" was their simple request. I told them I couldn't bear to look outside at the backyard anymore and the deck needed help. This was a breakthrough. I was finally able to articulate a need and delegate it. A small group of friends (many of whom were avid gardeners) came over with shovels and a power washer. In two and a half hours, my backyard had been transformed. The calla lilies were in bloom again. To celebrate, I provided lunch and cookies as a thank you gift.

Two things happened that day. I gave myself permission to receive help and my circle of friends experienced the joy of helping someone in need. Don't be afraid to ask for help and support.

Make a list of stuff that you need done because you lack the energy and tell someone who wants to be of service. Lotsa Helping Hands (https://lotsahelpinghands.com/) is a great online tool to let people know about projects that need to be done, food that would be appreciated, and times you want companionship or rides to appointments or errands. So many ask what they can do to help. Share your wish list with them. It could be a match for your needs and their desire to assist.

6. Counseling Is a Good Thing

For some reason, there is still a lingering stigma in some social groups surrounding therapy and counseling. For some older adults, seeing a therapist or counselor is akin to admitting you have a serious mental illness. Nothing could be farther from the truth. Of course, many of us are genetically disposed to certain mental illnesses and some people are in need of serious clinical intervention and behavior modification. But even for those who have no need for counseling in the course of their "normal" life can benefit from counseling while in grief. Everyone who is grieving a loved one needs personal tools to figure out a healing plan. It's a sign of strength to ask for assistance, especially with emotional issues.

Counselors provide tools to strengthen and improve our lives. Think of it. If you were stuck in a cavern or a hole deep in the earth and someone had the tools to pull you up to the surface, wouldn't you want that? That's what counseling does; it pulls us out of the hole, puts us back on terra firma and equips us with new strategies to heal and begin again. You don't have to commit to counseling forever, but it's a great idea to attend long enough to address the loss. Even if you don't think you need it, check in with a counselor anyway to get a sense of what to expect in the coming months. They can offer a baseline of where to start and help you figure out if you are providing yourself with the self-care you deserve.

7. Kids Grieve Too

Children grieve differently than adults and they often mourn silently. It's not unusual for a child to begin to make their bed and clean up after a death. They want to be the perfect child when they were previously a little less than perfect. Some will experience strong emotions and then take a break, laughing and playing games. Many assume that the death was their fault or that if they just do everything right, their loved one will return. Two things are important when helping a child deal with loss: (1) Allow them to talk things out with a trusted parent, friend, teacher, relative, or counselor without you. Arrange for them to see a counselor or a support group with a trained leader when they are ready or if they begin behaving erratically, particularly in a way that is counter to his or her personality, and (2) be available when they need you. They need a safe place to speak their heart and get it all out without guilt. Acknowledge whatever it is they're feeling and give them time alone when they ask for it. Answer the questions they ask in a way they can understand and be honest. Don't be abstract or vague or present a scholarly interpretation.

In Portland, there is an amazing place called The Dougy Center for children and their families. It is a safe place where children, teens, young adults, and their families who are grieving a death can share their experiences. In this wonderful old rambling house, kids can curl up on bean bags and rest, do art therapy, hang out with other kids who have suffered loss, meet one-on-one with therapists, or share their stories with a group of kids of similar ages and counselors. It is an oasis. Perhaps there is a center like it in your area.

If you have a child who is grieving, research what resources are available in your hospital or palliative care or hospice setting. Many facilities have anticipatory grief counselors or people that specialize in working with children before or after a death occurs. Give children safe places (summer camps, support groups, or one-on-one counseling) to unload their own baggage.

8. Be Good to Yourself

Most people who are working through various stages of grief fail to take care of themselves. Self-care is crucial during all stages of mourning.

In a Bad Way

I had one friend who refused to bathe, leave the house, or eat a full meal for almost a month after his loss. His energy was so low that he could barely pick up the phone to answer my calls, so I paid a visit. As I had suspected, the house was a mess and bills were on the counter unopened. This was not time to criticize but to listen. He told me his wife had handled everything—the bills, the house, and the social engagements. All he had to do was work and provide a salary. None of his relatives had called recently and only a few attended the memorial. His friends had stopped calling once he didn't return their initial messages left immediately after his wife's death. He was on a leave of absence from work and felt he had no meaning or purpose anymore. He didn't know where to start to address all the loss in his life. He felt as though he was leaving life on earth as he knew it and relocating to a foreign planet where he didn't know the language and no one knew how to translate.

I sat and listened for a while and then said, "So what are two things you need right now, and how can I make them happen for you?" His two requests were a home-cooked meal and someone to come over and watch sports on TV with him. I said I could arrange that and I added that I would also have a crew come and clean the house and noted that I could help him sort out his bills as well. He looked at me as if he'd been heard. I didn't share a full list of grief counselors or recommend small groups to join or cleaning agencies to hire, or offer a to-do list of grieving tasks. That might come later. I just let him know someone cared. This small gesture let him know that in turn he might begin to care for himself.

The following are three areas to address in order to renew your energy and begin the healing process:

- *Mental.* Read books, solve puzzles, or engage in hobbies.

- *Social/Emotional.* Build relationships, learn to laugh again, and attend social events.

- *Spiritual.* Pray, meditate, journal, or connect with your inner spirit or faith.

Self-care can take many forms. Sometimes self-care is a walk in the morning hours basking in the smells and sounds of nature. It might be a trip to the gym or spa, meditation or prayer, reading, enjoying a favorite hobby, traveling to a place of peace and comfort, or a personal retreat. Or self-care could be simply getting up each morning to shower and dress in clean clothes. Self-care is the things you do for yourself to recharge the inner soul and replenish the spirit, which is often weary from the stress and loss you have experienced.

I encourage people to make sure to do at least one thing for themselves each day and to plan for one thing they want to do on the weekend. This gives you something to look forward to. You can do these things by yourself, and as you feel more ready to reenter social circles, you may share these things with others. Take a hike, go on a bike ride, watch a movie, play a sport, cook a special healthy meal, or do a favorite craft. You may want to get involved in a service project that is meaningful to you. Many find that serving others gets the focus off the difficult things they are experiencing while helping another. Your endorphins will thank you.

And if you haven't already done so, try journaling. You don't have to let anyone see it. Just get the day out on paper. Write about your dreams, your frustrations, your prayers, and your hopes. In my toughest, most difficult times, I have always turned to journaling, and when I look back to those pages years later, I can see how God carried me through those times. I listed angry moments, observations, poems, and emotional insights. In my private journals, I could scribble down dark expletives in ALL CAPS and no one could see them. It is one of the most freeing exercises of expression. Get yourself a blank book or write on your laptop. Just make sure your journal is something portable and keep it close to you. Write it all down.

9. Tending to Your Physical Body

Grief can take a tremendous toll on your body. It increases inflammation, batters the immune system, and leaves you vulnerable to infection. It can increase blood pressure and the risk of blood clots. Intense grief can even alter the heart muscle so that it causes "broken heart syndrome," a form of heart disease with the same symptoms as a heart attack.[25] Add to those problems the headaches, dry mouth, stomach pain, nausea, loss of appetite or fatigue and you may not want to socialize or respond for a while. If you suffer from other common ailments like shortness of breath, you need to call your doctor. And if there is chest pain, you need to call 911. Rumination, or repetitive, negative, self-focused thoughts, is a way you can avoid problems, but it blocks the natural abilities of the body and mind to integrate new realities and heal. And if you have lost your role as a caregiver, the emotional demands of caregiving can leave you feeling depleted even before the death, and then with a lost sense of purpose after a person dies.

So what can you do when your body feels exhausted or depleted? Common remedies include exercising, getting enough sleep, and talking and socializing with family and loved ones who know you and can help with physical and mental health. Spend some time in nature and take the walk in a forest that replenishes your soul. Take time to retreat to a special place that encourages creativity or joy and plan small rewarding activities with friends. But if you are in a complicated grief (a persistent or pervasive grief that does not get better naturally) or depression (persistent low mood or agonizing feelings) or feel suicidal, it may be hard to reach out. Allow friends to come alongside and get the professional help required for your condition. Trying to distract yourself or push away your feelings only prolongs the process of healing. Lean into your grief and address it. It does go away eventually.

10. Rekindle Your Spiritual Life

We live in an era of fewer churches, temples and mosques and more "individual spirituality" centers. As a chaplain in a large medical center in California, the typical answer I hear when I ask people about their faith background is "I'm spiritual, not religious." You may not want to be affiliated with any institutional religion and prefer to seek your own path to find meaning and purpose. You might look to nature, science, or individual practices of ritual, prayer, or combinations of multiple religions that bring joy. You may also have what I call an embedded faith—the faith you grew up in. But depending on your experience, you may have abandoned that faith during your teen or young adult years. You may not want to return to religion as you face your mortality or that of a loved one. Or you may already be traditionally religious and be involved in a faith or religious community, finding deep connection with the people who know you and symbiotically care for you.

The spiritual life of people in North America is a very eclectic landscape and one not easily analyzed. What is true in my experience is that everyone has a spiritual core. When death occurs, many people want to know where their loved one is, or where they themselves might be going after life. These are good questions.

Spirituality gives life meaning and purpose. It provides a means to forgive and ask for forgiveness, to love, and to hope. It has the power to allow for transcendence, to help us rise above whatever circumstances come our way. It can help reconcile relationships, realize self-worth, resolve guilt, and create a stronger relationship with a higher being. In short, it takes the metaphysical and brings it down to earth level. It tries to explain the unimaginable, even the unspeakable.

Where do we begin to explore our spirituality when we need it most? Begin at the beginning. Before the daily grind of your life took over, what was it that brought you joy and renewal? What experiences in your life are most important or meaningful to you now? Where are your significant relationships? What values are most important to you? What gives you strength? What fears or worries are you experiencing and what hopes do you have? What goals are you setting for the future? To change the landscape of your loss, what needs must be met? Organized religions have all sorts of answers and holy books for these questions, but you will have to formulate meaning on your own.

Whatever your background or spiritual affiliation, work on finding meaning and purpose, the things that inspire you. Be fearless, and discover what brings intense joy back into your life and pursue it. Loss can suck the very life out of you. Spirituality and taking time to tap into God or something beyond yourself revives the soul. Identify what it is that wakes you up in the morning and gives you a reason to keep going. It is prayer, meditation, yoga, or guided imagery tapes? Is it thinking about vacation or a celebration in the future? Once you've begun to ponder those questions, it's a good time to seek some help and counsel. This is not time to be a lone ranger. You will need help. The following section is about some places to begin to craft the next chapter of your life.

Finding the Help and Assistance You Need

You will need help on your journey through grief, and there are many places you can find it. It's priceless to have a safe group of friends and counselors whom you see regularly for accountability and friendship. Here I detail some places to start.

As I noted previously, counseling can be invaluable during mourning. Look into your health care plan. Do they provide therapists who specialize in grief counseling? How many sessions do they offer for this type of therapy? This is a cost-effective way to begin and to find a person who can take your emotional temperature.

Ask for mental health care recommendations from friends and see if any of their suggestions match up with the counseling panel provided by your health care plan. If not, check on affordability and accessibility for you and decide what your budget can handle.

Research hospice and palliative care agencies and services. It's actually a requirement for hospice and palliative care agencies to provide 13 months of support for families after a death. Generally led by skilled professionals who understand complex forms of grief, these services are especially geared toward families of caregivers who need some relief and solace. Take advantage of this opportunity if offered. If it's not a fit, move on to other options.

Contact your local hospital about support. Similar to hospice, many hospitals provide grieving groups as part of after-care. If not, ask for a list of resources of possible counselors and counseling centers. Check with both your health plan and your hospital or hospice about children's programs. Many of the anticipatory grief counselors continue counseling with children after a death or suggest additional counselors outside the hospital. In addition, be sure to check for camps for children who have experienced loss. Having a week away to check in with other kids and hear their stories has the potential to lighten a burden from a child's life.

Many large religious centers align themselves with counseling groups or have on-site therapists to assist members of the community. Call the person in charge of congregational care and ask for their ideas. They may provide a weekly support group as well as one-on-one counseling.

Check in with community centers for their recommendations. As grief is often experienced by people losing a spouse after a long-term relationship, many senior centers offer the services of counselors and groups at no or low cost. Community centers also often have counselors available through the county who come on certain days of the week and make themselves available, or they may simply provide a list of resources of suggested counselors. Caseworkers are often the most reliable resource for this. Social workers and caseworkers are often called upon to provide a suggested list of centers and support groups for recently bereaved families.

Consider local counseling teams. In my community in the Bay Area, for example, there is a local board of trained and volunteer grief counselors called Kara (https://kara-grief.org/). On a sliding scale, they offer both one-on-one sessions and groups in a community center. As always, ask your friends what groups they found helpful and pursue what works for you. In the appendix, there is an extended list of websites and links for additional counseling resources.

Parting Thoughts/Last Words

"The journey of a thousand miles begins with a single step."

—Lao Tzu

You accomplished the first step in your journey by reading this book, and during this journey I hope you've had a chance to ponder who you are and learned how to talk with loved ones about specific housing and care wishes; to prepare yourself to navigate the halls of a hospital and be an advocate for yourself; to discover what a continuum of care is and wrestle with finding all your financial and legal data. I also hope you have learned creative ways to support and come alongside people who are ill, and what to expect when a person dies. And finally, if you have lost someone dear to you, I sincerely hope you have collected some helpful ideas on how to piece your life back together in the rebuilding process of grief and self-care.

But all of these things are just words on a page without action. As you finish this book, think about how you plan to accomplish your own personal end-of-life objectives. This process is a marathon, not a sprint. Take the time you need to gather your thoughts and emotions, plot out the specific tasks you need to do within a comfortable timeline, and then get to work. Your heirs will thank you.

You've made the journey. I hope you continue to nurture your soul and spirit as you enter the next chapter of your life. I am thankful to have been along for the ride.

*"When you were born, you cried and the world rejoiced.
Live your life so that when you die, the world cries and you rejoice."*

—Cherokee proverb[26]

Appendix

Resources

Chapter 1: Explaining and Expressing Meaning and Purpose

Books

Lamott, Anne. *Plan B: Further Thoughts on Faith*. New York: Riverhead Books, 2005.

Pantilat, Steven Z. *Life after the Diagnosis: Expert Advice on Living Well with Serious Illness for Patients and Caregivers*. Boston: DeCapo Press, 2017.

Thibault, Jane Marie, and Richard L. Morgan. *Pilgrimage into the Last Third of Life: 7 Gateways to Spiritual Growth*. Nashville: Upper Room Books, 2012.

Chapter 2: Making Wishes Known to Loved Ones

Books

Dunn, Hank. *Hard Choices for Loving People*. Naples, Florida: Quality of Life Publishing, 2009.

Kondo, Marie. *The Life-Changing Magic of Tidying Up: The Japanese Art of Decluttering and Organizing*. Berkeley, California: Ten Speed Press, 2017.

Products

Go Wish Cards, CODA Alliance, 950 Bascom Ave.,
    Suite 1113, San Jose, CA 95128, www.codaalliance.org,
    codaalliance@sbcglobal.net

Have the Talk of a Lifetime cards, Funeral and Memorial
    Information Council (FAMIC), 1-800-228-6332,
    talkofalifetime.org

Websites

The Conversation Project: conversationproject@ihi.org

eMedicare: Medicare.gov

Financial Planning Association:
    www.financialplanningassociation.org

IHSS: this is done by county in the state where you live.
    For California, the website is cdss.ca.gov/in-home
    -supportive-services.

Legacy Project video program and online questions:
    www.ucsflegacyproject.com

Life Interview Guide: https://brendon.com or download the
    PDF at https://brendon.com/wp-content /uploads/2016/06
    /LifeInterviewQuestions.pdf

National Alliance for Caregiving: www.caregiving.org,
    1-301-718-8444, info@caregiving.org

Stanford Letter Project: https://med.stanford.edu/letter.html

StoryCorps: www.storycorps.org

VetsAssist Program: https://veteranshomecare.com

What Matters Now: www.whatmattersnow.org,
    1-877-365-5533, info@whatmattersnow.org

Chapter 3: Talking about Health and Illness

Books

Cleland, Marilyn, Vicki L. Schmall, Marilynn Studervant, Leslie Congleton, Kay Kirkbride, Jean McFalls, Kathy Shannon, Virginia Sponsler, and Howard Turner. *The Caregiver Helpbook: Powerful Tools for Caregivers*. 2nd ed. Legacy Caregiver Services, 2006.

Department of Health and Human Services and Centers for Medicare and Medicaid Services *Medicare and You, 2021: The Official U.S. Government Medicare Handbook*. Baltimore, Maryland, 2020. (Available for download at https://www.medicare.gov/forms-help-resources/medicare-you-handbook/download-medicare-you-in-different-formats)

Goldberg, Sara. *How to Be a Patient*. New York: Harper Wave/Harper, 2019.

Harrold, Joan, and Joanne Lynn. *Handbook for Mortals: Guidance for People Facing Serious Illness*. New York: Oxford University Press, 1999.

Meyer, Maria M. *The Comfort of Home: An Illustrated Step-by-Step Guide for Caregivers*. 2nd ed. Portland, Oregon: Care-Trust Publications, 2002.

Roizen, Michael F., and Mehmet C. Oz. *YOU: The Owner's Manual, Updated and Expanded Edition: An Insider's Guide to the Body That Will Make You Healthier and Younger*. New York: William Morrow, 2012.

Forms

Power of Attorney for Health Care (indexed by state): www.powerofattorney.com

https://www.aarp.org/caregiving/financial-legal/free-printable-advance-directives

https://.fivewishes.org (honored in 42 states)

HIPAA: Authorization for Use or Disclosure of Health Information http://www.eforms.com/release/medical-hipaa

POLST forms (must be signed by a physician; please check the map to make sure the form is honored in your state): www.polstorg/map.form

National Hospice and Palliative Care Organization: www.nhpco.com

Chapter 4: Putting Your House in Order

Books

Clifford, Denia. *Plan Your Estate*. Berkeley, California: Nolo Press, 2018

Cullen, Melanie. *Get It Together: Organize Your Records So Your Family Won't Have To*. Berkeley, California: Nolo Press, 2018.

Final Wishes: When I'm Gone, My Info, Wishes, and Thoughts, The Write It Down Series. Journals Unlimited, 2013.

I'm Dead, Now What? Important Information about My Belongings, Business Affairs, and Wishes. White Plains, New York: Peter Pauper Press, 2015.

Websites
End-of-life planning

Cake: https://www.joincake.com

Lantern: https://www.lantern.co

New Narrative Memorials: https://www.newnarrative.ca

Parting: http://www.parting.com

Willing: https://willing.com

Financial and legal inventories

Canopy: https://www.canopyltc.co/

Mint by Intuit: http://www.mint.intuit.com

Legal information

Legal zoom: www.legalzoom.com

Nolo Press: www.nolo.com

Military/veterans

Burial flags: https://www.va.gov/burials-memorials
/memorial-items/burial-flags/

Service records: www.archives.gov/veterans/military-service
-records/

Chapter 5: Saying Goodbye and the Dying Process

Books

Byock, Ira. *Dying Well: The Prospect for Growth at the End of Life*. New York: Riverhead Books, Penguin and Putnam, 1997.

Byock, Ira. *The Four Things That Matter Most*. New York: Simon and Schuster, 2014.

Groves, Richard, and Henriette Anne Klausser. *The American Book of Living and Dying: Lessons in Healing Spiritual Pain*. Berkeley, California: Celestial Arts, 2005.

Hamilton, Joan. *When a Parent Is Sick: Helping Parents Explain Serious Illness to Children*. Lawrencetown Beach, Nova Scotia: Pottersfield Press, 2007.

Websites

American Music Therapy Association: www.musictherapy.org, 1-301-589-3300, info@musctherapy.org

Caring Bridge: www.caringbridge.org, 1-651-789-2300, customercare@caringbridge.org

Threshold Choir: www.thresholdchoir.org

Chapter 6: Figuring Out What Happens Next

Books

Lewis, C. S. *A Grief Observed*. London: Faber and Faber, 1961.

Smith, Harold Ivan. *Grief Keeping: Learning How Long Grief Lasts*. New York: Crossroad Publishing, 2004.

Websites

GatheringUS: www.gatheringus.com

LifeWeb360: www.lifeweb360.com

New Narrative: https://www.newnarrative.ca

Reimagine: www.LetsReimagine.org

Chapter 7: Piecing Things Back Together after Death: Conversations around Grief and Loss

Books

Williams, Litsa. "Before the Five Stages Were the Four Stages of Grief." August 28, 2013, https://whatsyourgrief.com /bowlby-four-stages-of-grief/.

GriefShare. *Your Journey from Mourning to Joy*. Wake Forest, North Carolina: Church Initiative, 2011. (This workbook is part of a 13-week course developed for people in churches who are working through the loss of a loved one.)

Kübler-Ross, Elizabeth. *On Death and Dying: What the Dying Have to Teach Doctors, Nurses, Clergy, and Their Own Families*. New York: Scribner, 2014.

Worden, J. William. *Grief Counseling and Grief Therapy*. New York: Springer Publishing, 2008.

Wright, Norman H. *Crisis and Trauma Counseling*. Ventura, California: Regal Books, 2003.

Websites

AARP: http://www.aarp.org/grief and loss (AARP has a toll-free grief line. In addition, they offer articles on practical matters, coping and community resources.)

Children (formerly The Center for Grieving Children): https://upliftphilly.org (This site is a resource for teachers, parents, counselors, and other adults who care for children.)

The Dougy Center: http://www.dougy.org (These articles are written to address the needs of teens' and children's grief.)

Grief Healing: http://www.griefhealing.com (Articles, discussion groups, and blog on how to deal with the loss of a loved one or a beloved pet.)

Headspace: www.headspace.com (This is a mindfulness mobile app.)

Lotsa Helping Hands: www.lotsahelpinghands.com (Assists people in organizing and reminding friends and family of the need for meals, chores, rides, or general assistance.)

Too Damn Young: www.toodamnyoung.com (This site is for teens and young adults navigating grief.)

Crisis Lines

Crisis Text Line: Text HOME to 741-741

Disaster Distress Helpline: 1-800-985-5990

National Suicide Hotline: 1-800-273-8255 (273-TALK)

Veterans Crisis Line: 1-800-273-8255, then press 1

▰▰▰ Questionnaire: What Matters Most to Me? ▰▰▰

1. What matters most to me? (*What comes to mind first when I read this question? For example, is it my spouse or partner, family such as my children and grandchildren, my faith, my profession, my friends, a cause? When I read this list, which response resonates most for me?*)

2. What brings me joy? (*What wakes me up in the morning? What inspires me to keep going each day? What are the tasks, programs, activities I love? What restores me? What brings me hope?*)

3. What do I hate/I avoid?

4. What has helped me in the past to get through difficult times? (*What are my best coping mechanisms? Is it sleep/rest, avoidance, prayer, checking in with family, asking loved ones for help, calling a friend, trying something new such as a new hobby or skill, exercising, cooking, walking, or what?*)

5. Are there upcoming milestones (anniversaries, birthdays, graduations, vacations, births, celebrations) or dates that are important for me to be present for or important events I want to attend?

6. Who depends on me? What kind of things do I provide for those people? Are there other people who can take on these responsibilities if I am no longer here?

7. What scares me right now? (*What keeps me up at night?*)

8. What are the things I want people to know about me? (*Or in the words of Anne Lamott, what makes me "truly, entirely, wildly, messily, marvelously" who I was "born to be"?*)

9. What am I on earth? What is my purpose?

10. If I get through this time, what would I like to change about me, my life, my community, my world?

▰▰▰ Questionnaire: What Are My Goals of Care? ▰▰▰

1. What is my current understanding of where I am with my illness? (*What have you heard already from your health care team? What have you learned from the internet or friends and family? What is your current understanding of what is happening to your body?*)

2. What has the doctor communicated with me so far? (*Has the doctor actually shared a prognosis or what is likely to happen? Have they communicated the kind of therapeutic options that are part of their plan of care?*)

3. How much more information about my current condition and future prognosis would I like to have? What do I want to know? What do I need to know? (*In some cultures, a patient is never told what is happening; information is only shared with a point person, such as the eldest child in the family, who then decides what the patient needs to know. What are your cultural beliefs about knowing and sharing difficult information?*)

4. What are my biggest fears and worries? (*Are you scared that you won't be able to care for others [children or a spouse] physically or financially? Are you scared to lose control? Are you frightened of being in pain or suffering physically? Are you worried about being a burden or lingering too long?*)

5. What gives me strength as I think about the future and my health concerns or illness? (*Is it your family or friends, faith or religion, a support group, or specific activities, like travel, reading, writing, gardening, or socializing with family and friends?*)

6. Which abilities are so critical to my life that I cannot imagine living without them? (*Is it being able to communicate with others? Are they walking, driving, and living at home alone? Is it taking care of your activities of daily living [ADLs] such as feeding, toileting, and dressing yourself?*)

7. If my health situation worsens, what's most important to me? (*Do you want to achieve an important life goal that you have not yet accomplished? Is it important for you to have mental awareness above all else? Do you want to do all you can to protect and support your family? Is it most important for you to be at home as long as possible, be physically comfortable as long as possible, or to be independent?*)

8. If I become sicker, how much am I willing to go through for the possibility of gaining more time? (*Do you want to avoid some procedures or treatments if their benefit is not substantial? Are you willing to be on a ventilator, live in a nursing home, endure physical discomfort or severe pain, spend time in the ICU, undergo invasive tests or procedures, or have a feeding tube?*)

9. How much does my health care proxy/durable power of attorney agent (see pages 77–80) or family know about my wishes and priorities?

Checklist of Essential Information and Documents

You can use the following list as a table of contents for your own binder or online archive of information:

I. **Financial Information**

   Inventory of Assets and Liabilities

   Insurance Policies: Life, Long-Term Care, Auto, and
      Homeowners

   Additional Income Sources: Social Security, Pension
      Plans, Wages, and Employment Accounts

   Retirement Plans

   Individual Retirement Accounts (IRAs) and Roth IRAs

   After-Death Arrangements: Burial, Cremation,
      Memorial and Funeral Rites, Organ Donation,
      Ecoburial, etc.

   Outstanding Debts and Regular Ongoing Bills

   Tax Documents

II. **Legal and Estate Information**

   The Will

   Trust Documents

   Durable Power of Attorney (POA) for Finances

   Durable Power of Attorney (POA) for Health Care,
      Advance Directive for Health Care, HIPAA
      authorization, and POLST

III. Other Information

    Military Service Information

    Personal Wishes and Gifts

    Pets

IV. Original Documents

V. User ID, Passwords, PINs, Codes, etc.*

    * KEEP THIS INFORMATION IN A SEPARATE PLACE

Body Disposition and
Memorial Planning Worksheet

Name: _____

Address: _____

_____

_____

Phone: _____

E-mail: _____

Emergency contact/point person(s) /personal representative(s)
to carry out wishes:

Phone: _____

E-mail: _____

Additional Information for Death Certificate

Full legal name _____

Mother's maiden name _____

Father's name _____

Date of birth _____

Place of birth_____

Social Security number location _____

Military record/honorable
discharge number _____

Medicare number, if any_____

Location of funds to pay for burial/memorial_____

_____

☐ I wish to be an organ donor. Location of advance directive or verification is:

☐ I wish to participate in whole body donation. Attach agreement with institution/hospital.

Body Disposition Wishes

Name of mortuary, crematorium, other agency _____

_____

Location (of interment, inurnment, other) _____

_____

Contact, if known _____

Other body preparation/process information (cremation, burial, embalming, special washing/preparation, eco burial options, family burial site, special clothes)

_____

_____

Casket preference (if any) _____

Cremains container preference (if any) _____

Headstone or marker specifications _____

Epitaph to read _____

_____

If cremation, scattering information: _____

_____

Company and location of airline/flight program/telephone of contact _____

Company and location of boat/telephone of contact _____

_____

County number for location of scattering cremains over public grounds _____

_____

Other _____

_____

_____

If interment or inurnment, plot purchased/reserved?

_____

Location _____

Agency or funeral home and address _____

_____

_____

Phone of agency _____

Contact _____

Attach copy of contract/payment.

Any other specific provisions?_____

_____

Military information_____

Military discharge Number/DD214_____

Military branch/rank/time served _____

_____

Preferred national burial site_____

Address _____

_____

_____

Phone _____

Ceremony/Program Preferences

Religious affiliation _____

Is a religious service desired? _____

What denomination if not listed above? _____

Is a military service desired? _____

If not, is a flag desired for ceremony? _____

Preferred facilitator (pastor, imam, rabbi, priest, etc.) to perform ceremony? _____

Specific personal/family wishes to be followed? _____

_____

Specific clothing to be worn for open casket? _____

_____

Specific flowers for casket or used in interment ceremony?

_____

Where will family be seated? _____

How many chairs/seats need to be reserved? _____

Pre-burial services

Will there be a viewing? _____

Location and time? _____

Will there be a wake at a private home? _____

Location and time? _____

Will there be a rosary performed at the parish? _____

Will body be present? _____

Open casket or closed? _____

Preferred location of memorial ceremony? _____

Transportation

Who will provide transportation? Funeral home? Private cars?

_____

Memorial preferences

Is memorial service or funeral private/invitation only?_____

Is memorial service open to public? _____

Location and time? _____

Music before ceremony/prelude? _____

Specific stories/anecdotes to be shared (*please attach copy*)

Sermon/message _____

_____

Special music_____

Solos _____

Instrumental _____

Sung _____

Group/congregational singing/hymns

_____

_____

Prayers/readings (scriptures, poems, etc.)

_____

_____

Eulogy speakers

Friends_____

_____

_____

Business/professional associates

_____

_____

_____

Family members

_____

_____

_____

Processional with family? _____

Recessional with family? _____

Music after ceremony/postlude? _____

Flowers at the ceremony (kind, color, provided by whom)

_____

_____

_____

Graveside ceremony preferences _____

_____

_____

Pallbearers. How many needed? _____

Name those who you would like to include for this role.

_____

_____

_____

_____

_____

_____

Place _____

Officiant _____

Special prayers, readings, speaker, eulogy? _____

_____

_____

Additional flowers for casket or niche? _____

_____

Reception preferences

Place _____

Charitable organization (for donations in lieu of flowers):

_____

Food requests _____

_____

_____

Seating arrangements (open, tables, etc.) _____

Slide show prepared (location of files and contact person or family archivist)_____

Memorabilia (photos, awards, recognition certificates, scrapbooks, pieces of clothing or uniforms, collages, or posters) prepared (location of files and contact or family archivist)

_____

_____

Overall

In this ceremony/program, I want people to know the following: _____

_____

Eulogy and Obituary Planning Worksheet

The following information will form a basis for your eulogy at the memorial service and the obituary for the newspaper, funeral home website, or house of worship notice.

Legal name _____

Date of birth _____

Place of birth (hospital, city, country)_____

_____

Name of mother (maiden name)_____

Profession _____

Name of father _____

Profession _____

Name(s) of siblings and age(s)

_____

_____

_____

_____

Address _____

Baptism /special ritual date (if applicable) _____

Officiant _____

Pre-school/elementary/middle school (activities, sports, music, theatre, special talents, friends, vacations)

_____

_____

_____

High school, including location and date of graduation (subjects studied, sports, mentors, special talents, vacations, friends, special events, honors, scholarships)

_____

_____

_____

College/community college/technical/graduate or professional school including location(s) and date(s) of graduation

_____

_____

_____

Majors/minors, mentors, sports, friends, special events, honors, scholarships/fellowships, awards

_____

_____

_____

Name (s) of spouse(s)/partner(s) and date(s) of marriage(s)

_____

_____

_____

Name of children's and date(s) of birth(s)

_____

_____

_____

Career (first and significant jobs/positions/promotions, including location, with what company/agency/group/school, special accomplishments)

_____

_____

_____

Military branch/rank/time served

_____

_____

_____

Volunteer/charitable work including location, with what organization/agency/group

_____

_____

_____

Special accomplishments/awards

_____

_____

_____

Travel/vacations

_____

_____

_____

Fun/recreation

_____

_____

_____

What do you want to be remembered for? What matters to you? What are your passions? _____

_____

_____

_____

Other important matters to mention/wisdom/last words

_____

_____

_____

Date of memorial?_____

Place: _____

Charitable organization (for donations in lieu of flowers): _____

_____

_____

Religious and Cultural Considerations

My hope is that this information may prove helpful to those visiting seriously ill patients or planning a burial, funeral rites, or memorial. This is not an exhaustive discussion, covering every religion, but I have attempted to cover the religions that constitute the largest groupings globally. For additional information on other religions and traditions, visit "Funeral Customs" by religion, ethnicity and culture at www.funeralwise.com.

As a caveat, I want to explain that I do not claim that this material is a comprehensive discussion of death and the major religions. Instead it is the result of my personal exploration of this topic and my experience as an interfaith chaplain in a sizeable teaching hospital located in a large urban area in Northern California. To write this material, I researched six major global religious groups (Judaism, Catholicism, Protestantism, Hinduism, Buddhism, and Islam); I then handed the material I had drafted to a ritual director of a Jewish synagogue, a priest, a pastor (me), a Muslim chaplain, a Buddhist monk, and a practicing Hindu and asked them to review what I had written. I asked them to revise the material for me in an effort to help people who are not members of a given faith be sensitive in visiting others, whose faith is important to them, when they are seriously ill or dying.

Most importantly, in the absence of personal knowledge or information about another person's belief, I highly recommend that you seek out the guidance of a priest or elder(s) of the same faith as the patient. Specifics about an individual's end-of-life wishes, of course, depend on what the individual notes in their advance directive, where they and their family is located, if they adhere to specific community or regional practices or sub-faith practices, and their caste, age, sex, and place of residence and worship.

I present this content by religion alphabetically as follows: Buddhism, Christianity/Catholicism, Christianity/Protestantism, Hinduism, Islam, and Judaism. For each religion, I discuss pre-death, post-death, funeral rites, and mourning.

For additional information regarding religions and safe practices, please refer to "Practical Considerations and Recommendations for Religious Leaders and Faith-Based Communities in the Context of COVID-19," World Health Organization, 4/7/20, at

> https://www.who.int/publications/i/item/practical
> -considerations-and-recommendations-for-religious
> -leaders-and-faith-based-communities-in-the-context-of
> -covid-19?

Buddhism

Pre-death. The aim of Buddhist practice is to cultivate an open, peaceful mind and to prepare for the next life. The concept of merit is common to all Buddhist sects. It is appropriate to ask the family what preparations they would like to make to bring merit to the loved one. Positive karma (deed, work, or action) alleviates suffering and prepares the persona for the next birth. When a person is ill, family may wish to arrange with the patient's temple to offer food, robes, prayer ceremonies, or to sponsor a statue or other temple project. Ceremonies can be performed in the home or temple and blessed substances can be brought back from the temple to bring comfort to the patient. A person's state of mind at the time of death is believed to be crucial, so Buddhists make every effort to bring about a peaceful, harmonious atmosphere with prayers and chants. When it is clear death is near, a Buddhist family may wish to have monastic practitioners come to chant and pray for the loved one. *Phowa* (prayers that aid the transference of consciousness in the moment of death, which are part of Vajrayana or Tibetan Buddhism) is one kind of religious support.[27] (In addition to Vajrayana or Tibetan Buddhism, the other two major branches of Buddhism are Mahayana and Theravada.)

Post-death. Upon the passing of a loved one, it is preferred that the body of a practicing Buddhist not be touched for at least three to eight hours. Although this practice is attributed to Mahayanist traditions, the majority of Chinese Buddhists practice it as well. Monastic practitioners can be requested to chant during this time, and conversation around the deceased is discouraged to keep the focus on creating a peacefully directed rebirth. If death occurs in a hospital, it may be requested that all the machinery, monitors, and electronics be turned off. Cremation is the most common disposition practice, although a burial is allowed. Organ donation and autopsies are also allowed, but families may ask that autopsies be conducted after the soul has left the body, usually three or four days after death.

Funeral Rites. Buddhist funeral rites generally take place at a family home, funeral home, or Buddhist temple. An officiant, usually a monk, is present. When a wake is included as one of the end-of-death ceremonies, the mourners pay their respects to the deceased person and to the family before the funeral rites.

The family typically wears white, while mourners and friends might wear black or other (but not bright) colors. There may be a portrait of the deceased in front of the casket along with an image of Buddha and an altar with candles and other offerings such as flowers and fruit. Incense may be burned. There are no formal guidelines for the funeral service but they may include prayer, meditation, and possibly a message and a eulogy.[28] The body is typically cremated after the service. If it is cremated after a wake but before the funeral rites, there is a cremation service. In general, a Buddhist funeral is held within one week after death. In Chinese tradition, the location of interment may be important; a burial site on a higher location such as a hillside may be considered beneficial.

Mourning. Traditionally, families do not receive visitors until after the funeral. White flowers are an appropriate gift for the family. In the Tibetan Buddhist tradition, there are 49 days of specific prayers and practices after death with ceremonies on the seventh, forty-ninth, and hundredth day anniversaries of the death.[29] In addition, there are holidays where ancestors are remembered and prayers are recited and offerings are made at the temple.

Christianity/Catholicism

Pre-death. When a person is ill, two sacraments are often performed by a priest. Sacraments are Christian rites recognized as of particular importance and significance. One sacrament, reconciliation (also known as confession) is the act of obtaining completeness and wholeness with God. This sacrament reunites the soul to God and restores sanctifying grace to the soul. The second sacrament, anointing of the sick (previously known as "last rites"), is administered to anyone with a serious illness. This sacrament is given, for example, to a person before a major operation or to and elderly patient if their condition has weakened. An additional sacrament that may be performed is the Eucharist (Holy Communion), which is the ceremony that commemorates the Last Supper of Christ, in which bread and wine are consecrated and consumed. The Eucharist can be offered by a priest, deacon of the parish, or an "extraordinary minister" (a volunteer commissioned by the church). Family and friends may recite the rosary (a scripture-based prayer recited with prayer beads). Friends may also offer prayers and place prayer cards, a rosary, or scapular (a fabric piece representing a saint) on or near the ill patient. In addition, family and visitors often visit their church and light candles or pray on behalf of the patient. Euthansia is forbidden in the Catholic Church.

Post-death. If a Catholic priest is present at the time of death, they offer a prayer of commendation and consecration for the soul's journey to heaven. The family may remain with the deceased and pray over the body for the soul to be united with Christ in heaven. There are no specific requirements for washing or shrouding. Organ donation is justifiable. The Catholic Church still strongly recommends traditional burial, but it does not reject the process of cremation. Cremated remains are to be treated with the same dignity and respect traditionally given to the full body in a casket. The practice of scattering cremains on the sea, from the air, or on the ground, or keeping cremated remains in the home is not in keeping with this faith.

Funeral Rites. It is traditional in many Catholic communities to have a vigil service which may also be referred to as a wake or rosary service. Traditionally held the night before the funeral mass at the funeral home, this service is a time to pay respect to the decedent and the family, and the family may choose to have an open or closed casket.

Typically on the day following the wake or vigil service, a funeral mass takes place in the parish church of the deceased where they have been receiving sacraments. A priest presides over the Mass and a procession brings the closed casket into the church. The funeral mass includes: sprinkling the casket with holy water; the draping of a pall (a cloth that symbolizes the white garment a person was given at baptism) over the casket; a procession; and the reciting of various blessings and readings from scripture by the family and priest. At this Mass, the Eucharist is celebrated, and the casket is incensed. The Mass ends with a recessional of the casket out of the church to the burial site.

After the funeral mass, the family and invited guests gather at the cemetery for a committal service and the priest says a final prayer before the casket is lowered into the ground or placed in the crypt. If the deceased has been cremated, a funeral Mass and a rite of committal are celebrated the same day. A reception may follow at the church, a private home, or restaurant, where mourners gather to share a snack or meal.

Mourning.[30] Some Catholic families choose to celebrate the deceased on the anniversary of their death or All Saints Day, celebrated on November 1. A tradition of the Latinx culture is *Dia de los Muertos*, (the Day of the Dead) when deceased ancestors are honored with a special altar and traditional dishes. Prayers are said to remember friends and family members who have died in order to support the spiritual journey of those who have passed away.

Christianity/Protestantism

Pre-death. In the hospital, families who are members of the various Protestant sects, may request a pastor, priest, or church elder pray over a seriously ill patient and anoint them with oil for healing in the tradition of James 5. In certain denominations, receiving Christ as the Lord and Savior is foundational to resurrection into heaven. Baptisms are permitted as well as a service to receive Christ into the heart or communion. Families may offer uplifting scriptures such as Psalm 23, Psalm 103, and selections from Revelation 21 and 22 and John 14. As is the case for people of many beliefs, songs or hymns and blessings as personal tributes to the patient are welcomed. Prayer services are common as well as moments of confession, forgiveness, and reconciliation for sins and apologies for any wrongdoings. At the moment of death, Protestants believe the soul rises into heaven and is received by Christ, reuniting with all the saints who have gone before them.

Post-death. In most Protestant denominations, organ donation or whole-body donation is permitted. The body is prepared as per hospital protocol and transferred to the family's choice of facility. Families typically plan a memorial and burial service a week to a month after the death depending on family and extended family schedules. In contemporary times, flowers may be discouraged in lieu of a memorial gift to a favorite charity of the deceased. Both cremation and casket burial are common for Protestants.

Funeral Rites. In the days leading up to the memorial and/or burial service, a family may have a viewing at the funeral home (a gathering at which the body is present and the casket is open) or a wake/gathering at a private home or both. These events sometimes span two or three days. The church memorial is a celebration of life, and in many denominations, the casket or cremains are absent. In other church's funerals, the casket or cremains may be present for the ceremony. The service normally consists of a prayer of welcome, opening hymn, prayers of thanksgiving, the Lord's Prayer, personal testimonies and tributes of the deceased, readings and scriptures, a message based on the scriptures read, a closing hymn, and a prayer of dedication to declare the soul is with God. If there is no service in a house of worship or church, then an abbreviated form of this service may be done graveside. The graveside service is normally attended by extended family and close friends and can be held in conjunction with the memorial service or before or after the memorial. It's customary to have a reception after the services either in the church or at the home of the family or friends.

Mourning. Families may choose to visit the burial site on the anniversary of death, on a birthday or wedding anniversary, or during the holidays, when extended family visits.

Hinduism

These are generally followed procedures for Hindus. As noted earlier, if you are unsure what a person's faith prescribes, seek the guidance of a priest or elders who are members of their same religious group. For people who practice all faiths, including Hinduism, specifics about an individual's end-of-life wishes depend on their advance directive, personal experiences, location, family of origin, caste, sex, and age.

Pre-death. In the final days before death, if a Hindu patient is at home, visitors, chanting, lighted lamps, photos of deities or other spiritual objects, music, and incense may be encouraged. The person may lie on or close to the ground. If the patient is in the hospital, depending on hospital protocol, it may not be possible to lower the bed close to the ground nor are incense and lighted lamps permitted. Soft chanting or music may provide solace. Like people of all faiths, a person who practices Hinduism who is preparing for death may feel that they have unfinished concerns or things they wish to say to significant others or they may wish to be relieved of a past guilt. When death is near, the patient may try to engage the mind in remembering the Lord by reciting his name and thinking of his glories. Visitors may wish to recite verses from the Vedas (sacred texts). If the mind is engaged in thinking of the Lord at the time of death, the person attains the ultimate abode of the Lord. When possible, a dying person may be given holy water from a sacred source such as the Ganges River.

Post-death. The concept of samskaras (sacraments) is foundational to Hinduism. The sixteen samskaras are performed from birth to death at important stages of life to represent purification and refining the mind, body and soul. After a person dies, the last or sixteenth samskara—*Antyeshti*—is performed by a person's survivor. *Antyeshti* funeral rites vary according to the caste and religious sect but generally involve cremation followed by disposal of the ashes in a sacred river if possible. Carrying out this final step allows the soul to be liberated from its bondage to the body.

Hospitals typically do not allow a wake or vigil of the body at the hospital, but if family members are unable to come to the hospital at time of death, there may be accommodation for a viewing of the deceased in a designated room. The hospital may not release the body to be taken home but may make arrangements for the deceased to be transferred directly from the room to a crematorium.

Funeral Rites. Most Hindu families choose cremation and some families may choose that the body be cremated in India. All rituals before and after cremation are typically performed exclusively by men. Donation of body parts such as eyes, kidneys, or the heart to other human beings prior to cremation is becoming a more acceptable practice among Hindus. As with any faith, a family or priest may have preferences about a cremation facility and mortuary as well as the services.

The final rites involve specific steps, as is the case with most religious rites in most religions. Mourners wear white cotton clothing to signify purity and peace, and the eldest son, husband or nearest male relative performs the service. The ceremony involves a priest reciting a verse for peace. Family and friends view the face of the deceased and pay their final respects. Mourners come home, bathe, and possibly sing prayers for peace of the departed soul. After two to three days, the ashes from the cremation are collected and placed in an urn. Ashes from the urn are immersed in a sacred moving body of water or the ocean either in the country where the person lived or in India. Scattering over land is uncommon.

Mourning. Typically a mourning period of 10–13 days is observed. A final ceremony is conducted to elevate the soul. Family and friends are invited to make gifts of food and money and multiple Gods are invoked. The final ceremony involves an offering of rice.

In many parts of India, people perform a ceremony on other specific days including the death anniversary. Others may visit a favorite restaurant of the deceased, some worship and pray, or family and friends might enjoy a simple meal at home together. More detailed information regarding end of life rituals may be found in *Last Rituals for the Indian American Community: A Resource Guide* by the Desai Foundation (thedesaifoundation .org/wp-content/uploads/2017/09/last-rituals-guide.pdf).

Islam

Pre-death. Before death, family members and close friends are present at the bedside of patients to help them turn their thoughts to God and remind them of the good deeds they did and about God's mercy and forgiveness in order that they might receive God's favor. An imam (religious leader) is typically called to pray with the family. The Qur'an is read.

The ill person may wish to face toward the northeast in the direction of Mecca where Muslims face for daily prayers. Family members may offer *dua* (supplication prayers) to God to help the patient's soul depart from the body. Death is viewed as a moment of submission to the Will of God. Crying as an expression of sadness is permissible, but wailing is not encouraged.

Post-death. Traditionally, Muslims wish to be buried within 24 hours or as soon as possible. The body is to be covered with a white sheet to maintain modesty and is to remain covered. Families may request that the body be transferred directly from the hospital to the place of preparation. Cremation is not allowed, but autopsies are allowed if deemed necessary. Family members often engage a funeral home in coordination with a local Islamic center for *janaza* (funeral) prayers after washing and shrouding. Muslims are encouraged to be buried locally where they die. *Ghusl* (full-body ritual purification) is performed and the body is wrapped in pieces of white cotton fabric, a shroud. Once the wrapping is completed, the body is placed inside the casket for burial.

Funeral Rites. Janaza (funeral) prayers are said at the funeral home or mosque. The body is escorted to the grave in silence. Prayers are said at the graveside. Each person participating takes three handfuls of dirt and throws it into the grave. When the grave is covered with dust, prayers are said to invoke God's mercy on the deceased. A farewell with a greeting of peace is offered to the deceased and all present.

Mourning. Friends and family are encouraged to provide food for the bereaved family for three days or more following the death. There are various schools of thought in Islam regarding mourning periods, but the deceased may be celebrated on the third, seventh, and fortieth days after death. It is common to give condolences to the family of the deceased, especially on the seventh day after the death of their loved one.[31]

Judaism

Pre-death. Prayers, tributes, legacies, blessings, and wishes may be offered around the bed, and a rabbi (spiritual leader/teacher) may be present. *Tshuvah* (atonement of sins and the mending of relationships with people and God) may also be encouraged as well as other prayers and a reading of the psalms.

Post-death. The rabbi is called to be informed of the death and in turn inform the congregation. A person is assigned to be the *shomer* (watchman) who stays with the deceased from the time of death until the funeral or burial. A designated group of people (*chevra kadisha*) perform the *T'harah* (ritual washing with flowing water) and the body is shrouded in linen and may be placed in a simple wooden, typically pine, box without any metal.

Funeral Rites. The funeral and burial are to take place as soon as possible after death but not on *Shabbat* (sabbath) or holy days. In most congregations, it is simply respectful to inter the body within "a reasonable amount of time" after death to avoid unnecessary delay. Embalming is discouraged as the body is to decompose naturally, and routine autopsies can be viewed as not acceptable as they violate respect for the body. Cremation is prohibited in the scriptures because the body is the property of God. However, it should be noted an increasing number of Jews, along with members of most other religions, do choose cremation. Depending on whether the deceased was from a Reform, Conservative, or Orthodox congregation, other rituals may be observed.

Depending upon a congregation's policy, a service may be held in the temple or synagogue promptly after the death. If a service is held, it is typically brief and includes a recitation of psalms, a memorial prayer, and a eulogy (an overview of a person's life and qualities) followed by a recessional. Some families choose not to have a service at the temple and opt for a graveside service at the cemetery. *Kriah*, the ancient tradition of standing and tearing or cutting one's clothes or cutting a black ribbon worn on one's clothes, is performed by the child, parent, spouse, and sibling of the deceased and is typically done at the funeral home before the funeral service begins. A cut is made on the left side of the clothing for parents, over the heart, and on the right side for all other relatives. It symbolizes the expression of grief and anger at the loss of a loved one. The torn or cut garment or ribbon is worn during the seven days of shiva, (but not on Shabbat or festival days and some continue this practice for the 30-day period of mourning.[32] At the cemetery, often a brief interment service is performed. The casket is lowered and covered. The mourners may participate in a ceremony known as filling the grave. The rabbi offers a brief prayer, "May _____ go to his/her place in peace" and then hands one of the principal family members a shovel or gestures for them to pick up a trowel and drop a little of the newly dug earth onto the coffin. Each member of the family is invited to take turns and either hand the shovel to the next person or put the shovel back into the earth for the family member to pick it up. After the immediate family has finished their turns, other mourners are invited to take a turn.[33] Then the memorial prayer and the *Kaddish* prayer are recited. The *Kaddish* (*Qaddish* or *Qadish* meaning "holy") is a hymn of praise about God and God's name and is a vigorous declaration of faith.

Mourning. A mourner's *Kaddish* is said as part of the rituals in all prayer services. Mourners say *Kaddish* to show that despite their loss they still praise God. *Kaddish* cannot be recited alone. Traditionally, Jews are required to say the *Kaddish* for 30 days after burial for a child, spouse or sibling, and for 11 months after burial for a parent.

Shiva (meaning "seven") is the seven-day mourning period immediately following the burial. During shiva, mourners may remain in the home and the Jewish community comes and offers comfort. A special memorial candle remains lit for the seven-day period and at the end of the morning prayers on the seventh day, the mourners symbolically reenter the world by taking a walk around the block.

Shloshim (meaning "thirty") is the 30-day period following burial. During the 23 days after shiva, the intensity of mourning in *shloshim* is reduced. However, some restrictions continue to remain in effect. This 30-day custom is reserved for the death of spouses, siblings, and children, the mourning period for parents is one year.

The *yahrzeit* is the annual anniversary of the death of a person. A 24-hour candle is lit the evening before the day of the *yahrzeit* as well as on other holidays. During these commemorations, people remember the deceased with introspection. A synagogue congregation may recite the name of the deceased whose *yahrzeit* is being observed. Some families also commemorate this anniversary with unveiling and dedication of the grave marker, although this can be done any time after the *shloshim*.[34]

HIPAA Authorization For Use or Disclosure Of Health Information

This form is for use when such authorization is required and complies with the Health Insurance Portability and Accountability Act of 1996 (HIPAA) Privacy Standards.

Print Name of Patient: _____

Date of Birth: _____ SSN: _____

1. My Authorization

I authorize the following using or disclosing party:

to use or disclose the following health information.

☐ All of my health information

☐ My health information relating to the following treatment or condition:

_____

☐ My health information covering the period from _____ to _____
                                                                    (date)   (date)

☐ Other: _____

The above party may disclose this health information to the following recipient:

Name (or title) and organization _____

Address _____

City _____ State _____ Zip_____

Phone _____ Fax _____ Email _____

The purpose of this authorization is (check all that apply):

☐ At my request

☐ Other: _____

☐ To authorize the using or disclosing party to communicate with me for marketing purposes when they receive payment from a third party to do so.

☐ To authorize the using or disclosing party to sell my health information. I understand that the seller will receive compensation for my health information and will stop any future sales if I revoke this authorization.

This authorization ends:

☐ On (date) _____

☐ When the following event occurs: _____

_____

II. My Rights

I understand that I have the right to revoke this authorization, in writing, at any time, except where uses or disclosures have already been made based upon my original permission. I may not be able to revoke this authorization if its purpose was to obtain insurance. In order to revoke this authorization, I must do so in writing and send it to the appropriate disclosing party.

I understand that uses and disclosures already made based upon my original permission cannot be taken back.

I understand that it is possible that information used or disclosed with my permission may be redisclosed by the recipient and is no longer protected by the HIPAA Privacy Standards.

I understand that treatment by any party may not be conditioned upon my signing of this authorization (unless treatment is sought only to create health information for a third party or to take part in a research study) and that I may have the right to refuse to sign this authorization.

I will receive a copy of this authorization after I have signed it. A copy of this authorization is as valid as the original.

Signature of Patient: _____

Date: _____

If the patient is a minor or unable to sign, please complete the following:

☐ Patient is a minor: _____ years of age

☐ Patient is unable to sign because: _____

_____

Signature of Authorized Representative: _____

Date: _____

Print Name of Authorized Representative: _____

Authority of representative to sign on behalf of the patient:

☐ Parent   ☐ Legal Guardian   ☐ Court Order

☐ Other: _____

III. Additional Consent for Certain Conditions

This medical record may contain information about physical or sexual abuse, alcoholism, drug abuse, sexually transmitted diseases, abortion, or mental health treatment. Separate consent must be given before this information can be released.

☐ I consent to have the above information released.

☐ I do not consent to have the above information released.

Signature of Patient or Authorized Representative:

_____

Date: _____ Time: _____

IV. Additional Consent for HIV/AIDS

This medical record may contain information concerning HIV testing and/or AIDS diagnosis or treatment. Separate consent must be given to have this information released.

☐ I consent to have the above information released.

☐ I do not consent to have the above information released.

Signature of Patient or Authorized Representative:

_____

Date: _____ Time: _____

Notes

1. "The Farewell: Culture's Role in How We Approach End-of-Life," The Conversation Project, January 6, 2020, https://theconversationproject.org/tcp-blog/the-farewell-cultures-role-in-how-we-approach-end-of-life/.

2. VJ Periyakoil, The Stanford Letter Project, 2015, https://med.stanford.edu/letter/what-matters-letter.html.

3. "43 Percent of U.S. Virus Deaths Are Tied to Nursing Homes and Long-Term Care Facilities," *New York Times*, June 29, 2020, https://www.nytimes.com/2020/06/29/world/coronavirus-updates.html?action=click&module=Top%20Stories&pghype=Homepae#link-c-785897.

4. The cost range of building an ADU 2016–2019 was $112,000–$285,000 and the average cost was $181,000. (2020, www.buildinganadu.com.)

5. "Providing Care and Comfort at the End of Life," National Institute on Aging, US Department of Health and Human Services, May 17, 2017, https://www.nia.nih.gov/health/providing-comfort-end-life.

6. Jim Chappelow, "Activities of Daily Living (ADL)," Investopedia.com, August 18, 2020, https://www.investopedia.com/terms/a/adl.asp.

7. "How Much Does Assisted Living and Home Care Cost in the US?" Seniorliving.org, October 28, 2019, https://www.seniorliving.org/assisted-living/costs/.

8. *Medicare and You 2021, The Official U.S. Government Medicare Handbook*, Center for Medicare and Medicaid Services, 2021, p.28.

9. US Department of Health and Human Services, 2015, https://aspe.hhs.gov/basic-report/what-lifetime-risk -needing-and-receiving-long-term-services-and-supports.

10. Based on average 2014 New York Life Cost of Care figures for 20 hours a week of home care at $22/hour, $4139 per month for a one-bedroom unit in an assisted-care facility in California and $95,707 per year for a private room in a nursing facility (AARP Long Term Care Options Letter, July 2019).

11. Peter Moore, "Broke from Cancer," *AARP Magazine*, July/August 2018, 55.

12. Ibid, 55.

13. Marie Kondo, The Life-Changing Magic of Tidying Up: The Japanese Art of Decluttering and Organizing (Berkeley: Ten Speed Press, 2017).

14. Welcome.storyworth.com

15. Lorie Konish, "This Is the Real Reason Most Americans File for Bankruptcy," CNBC, Personal Finance, February 11, 2019, https://www.cnbc.com/2019/02/11/this-is-the -real-reason-most-americans-file-for-bankruptcy.html.

16. The Five Wishes advance directive is available for $5 on their website at https://fivewishes.org/shop/order/product /five-wishes-advance-directive.

17. Jennifer Miller, "Boom Time for Death Planning," *New York Times*, July 21, 2020, https://www.nytimes.com /2020/07/16/business/boom-time-for-death-planning.html.

18. Ibid.

19. Ira Byock, *The Four Things That Matter Most: A Book about Living*. 10th anniversary ed. (New York: Simon and Schuster, 2014).

20. National Institute on Aging, "Providing Care and Comfort at the End of Life," National Institutes of Health, US Department of Health and Human Services, May 17, 2017. https://www.nia.nih.govhealth/providing-comfort-end-life.

21. *Encyclopedia Britannica Online*, s.v. "wake," accessed November 10, 2020, www.britannica.com/search?query =wake.

22. Shoshana Ungerleider, "Virtual Grieving: Is There Closure If There Is No Goodbye?" *San Francisco Chronicle*, April 14, 2020, https://www.sfchronicle.com/opinion/openforum /article/Virtual-grieving-Is-there-closure-if-there-is-no -15198399.php.

23. William Worden, *Grief Counseling and Grief Therapy: A Handbook for the Mental Health Practitioner* (New York, Springer Publishing Company, 2018).

24. Elisabeth Kübler-Ross, *On Death and Dying: What the Dying Have to Teach Doctors, Nurses Clergy and Their Families,* 50th edition, New York: Scribner, 2014.

25. Stephanie Hairston, "How Grief Shows Up in Your Body," WebMD, July 19, 2011, Webmd.com/special-reports/grief -stages/20190711/how-grief -affects-your-body-and-mind.

26. Sofo Archon, "26 Native American Quotes on Life and Death," *The Unbounded Spirit*, https://theunboundedspirit .com.

27. Marilyn Smith-Stoner, "Phowa: End of Life Ritual Prayers for Tibetan Buddhists," *Journal of Hospice and Palliative Nursing*, vol.8, no.6, November/December 2006, 357.

28. "Buddhist Funerals Guide," BurialPlanning.com, www.burial planning.com.

29. Marilyn Smith-Stoner, "End of Life Needs of Patients Who Practice Tibetan Buddhism," *Journal of Hospice and Palliative Nursing*, vol. 7, no. 4, July/August 2005, 233.

30. Amy Wolkenhauer, "Catholic Funeral Service: Mass, Traditions and What to Expect," Cake, January 15, 2020, https://www.joincake.com/blog/catholic -funeral-mass-tradtions-what-to-expect/.

31. Kamyar Hedayat, MD. Department of Pediatrics, Stanford University, "Death and Bereavement in Lecture, accessed June 28, 2014.

32. "The Basics of Kriah, or Tearing a Piece of Clothing," My Jewish Learning, 2002–2020, https://www .myjewishlearning.com/article/the-basics-of-kriah-or -tearing-a-piece-of-clothing/

33. Anita Diamant, "Filling the Grave," My Jewish Learning, 2002–2020, https://www.myjewishlearning.com/article /filling-the-grave/.

34. American Geriatric Society, *Doorway Thoughts: Cross-Cultural Health Care for Older Adults*, vol. 3 (Boston: Jones and Bartlett Publishers), 108–109.

Index